Why Do Turks Act Weird?

Mustafa Ugur Etike

Published by Mustafa Ugur Etike, 2024.

WHY DO TURKS ACT WEIRD?

First edition. January 29, 2024.

Copyright © 2024 Mustafa Ugur Etike.

ISBN: 979-8224405183

Written by Mustafa Ugur Etike.

WHY DO TURKS ACT WEIRD?

AN ESSAY ON THE NATURE OF ALIENATION AND CULTURAL DIFFERENCE

Introduction

*T*urkish people. A weird group of individuals. They are not used to being individuals of a nation; instead they would like to think that they are the subjects of a political entity owned by some higher powers. They invented the Turkish coffee (*Türk kahvesi*) 500 years ago, they have been drinking it since, with great pleasure and complicated traditional applications; however for the last 70 years they praise the tea (*çay*), meanwhile the coffee is being marginalized through Western use of filtration, milk and foam which is the liberal presentment of the drink in the Turkish eyes... They like animals, much more than they like their own kind sometimes, as they show it by letting big dogs roam freely around the streets, play games and when the game gets a little tense let them have some little fights; also they let them form packs, fight battles for territories as packs, eat each other or a random human kid: It is surprising how similar we and our animal friends are! As you know, the same animal-loving Turkish people sacrifice cattle, sheep and even chickens every eid al-adha (*kurban bayramı*), each family chooses a man and a woman to use their own hands, one to cut the throat of and other to skin the animal. So yes, the Turks; strange, funny...

Don't get any of this wrong, they like what they like, as much as they like their own and as a squirrel likes nuts; and they hate what they hate, as much as they hate their own, and sometimes, not even knowing why. And this essay is not about Turks entirely, but it is more about you, people who are not Turkish and find Turkish act weird time to time. Also the people who find not only Turkish funny, but can't comprehend *the other* concept totally.

Be sure and beware: All of our problems are arising from *being*. Yes, actively existing; and we know it. We know it very well. And when we can't prevent -mentally or physically reject- the existence, it creates a hole, an internal conflict... A paper showed that men are angrier when they are not able to express themselves properly. I see it and raise it: Humankind and all the crowds are easily agitable due to the unpleasant reality of life and not being able to explain what is happening to them properly. We have maladaptive daydreams about endless scenarios, struggles, achievements; yet we are caged into experiencing only a few of them.

We are born to die, our cells are dying and we are decaying until the new cells can't be replaced no more and dead ones pile up. Our neurons and hardly earned complex synaptic connections are betraying us; with the each minute passes we are forgetting more. Our immune system gives itself up and we are getting more likely to have cancer.

Besides anything lethal, life is good at destroying our joy too. Everything has a price: If you eat, you gain weight and it is now easier to gain weight than to lose it. Once in nature, eating more was better to survive, and finding more food than you can eat was actually terrific; but life didn't give you enough food then. The modern age has brought about technology, longer life, comfort, healthier standards and now we live 40 to 60 more years; so we can work for 40 to 60 more years. Maybe not lemons but life gave us dopamin to enjoy, but it put it somewhere safe and away in the top shelf, so every time we climb to reach it, we fall; which is what happens in life, we laugh a lot, to cry a lot the following day.

So yes, the *Turks*... They are not the cause of our problems, but our perspective on them, our perspective on *the other*, *the alien*, is. Maybe none of us should even be here, but we are. The hole in us, that is created by this distorted form of existence, make us stick to our basic programming: "Discriminate the other, run or fight!", meanwhile the only thing we don't discriminate is our primitive instincts. As weird gets weirder and the Turks become a symbol of utter confusion between hate and understanding for some people, the only solution to the pain and sorrow caused by our biased opinion is self-awareness.

We have lived long enough as fish, not being aware of the sea we are in. Thanks to the industrial revolution, locomotives, electricity, radio, television, internet, social media and much more, we are everywhere, we know what *others* do. Europe in 16th century still had the image of demonic Turkish soldiers as the signs of the apocalypse. Thanks to the various means of travel and tools of acquaintance, *others* have become less scary and more humane; and this was the first phase: To get to know and overcome one's primal instincts.

And as for the second one, we are learning about ourselves by learning about nature, comprehending that we are no different than any *other*, so the differences among cultures is nothing but a fake façade. Therefore *we are the other* and the Turks are weird as much as we are.

I hope this essay in the search for the sources of alienization -and normalization of the alien- help the reader discover the common ground with their own weird Turks, or *the other*.

MANIFESTATION OF NATURE

So when they continued asking him,
he lifted up himself, and said unto them:
"He that is without sin among you,
let him first cast a stone at her."
John 8:7

I am not sure if this inquiry about the unjust alienation of some people (by the people) satisfy your urge of being proud about your inner liberal stance, however I am very optimistic about my headings to pique your interest or at least confuse you. Pointing out that you have an "inner liberal stance" doesn't imply that we all don't have an "inner conservative stance"; where maybe the latter is more profound than the former.

A person who is questioning the *other*, should question oneself. Whether it is throwing stones or bitter words, pointing your index finger at someone will always make the other fingers show you. The eyes you are seeing from, or the body you are producing or receiving sounds from can't be watched or judged by yourself and it is always easier to bury your head in the sand. To you, you are the center; the camera is you and there is no third-person view as an option. You are not aware of how you look, how your gestures and facial expressions make people feel like and what natural signals others get consciously or unconsciously when you contact other people. Yet you have a lot of ideas and prejudices about you and your environment considering all the unknown.

The parts of the unknown have been explored throughout history. The first question was about the universe -also called nature- and existence and the "things around" -so basically, life. As one is not aware of oneself, it brings curiosity of the *other*; because one is the other, thus the only sensible explanation of living things are derived from the subjective perspective. The building block of life is identical for all living things; but most importantly, material source of all objects are the very same, whether they breathe or not. So this unconscious reductionist view made us question the nature of matter: If we are all matter, then why do we act differently than the other matter?

First things first; we know that any mass is full of space, and so are we. We are mostly empty, we interact with other masses, particles and waves in which some penetrates us -therefore love and science is similar. Everything is energy and we are no exception. As the famous saying goes: *We are bound by the laws of physics*. I claim a better one: We are the laws of physics. Because space-time is made of itself; there is no emptiness, but there are virtual particles, electromagnetic forces, relativistic time, entropy and so on... Everything is in space because space is everything. Each year we discover something new, something smaller and bigger than the previous, we define things by the rules of the cosmos and quantum world; we discover new parts to create a cleaner picture of the whole. So it is very normal for any researcher to think that humans are matter... To sum up, this understanding is the basis of the things around.

Understanding it or not, accepting it or not, we chose to create ourselves an artificial reality within this reality. We built reality: Politics, language, traditions, economy, professions and much more. We religiously trust in our system; we really think that there are doctors, teachers, engineers, as well as states and countries, and flags and anthems; meanwhile they are actually the social manipulations of the environment; we made them all. But what do we mean by "*we*"? Yes, we are a part of something bigger, but to evaluate this artificial reality and to have a philosophical outcome (or *truth* if you dare), we must agree with the terms of artificiality.

Obviously we are sharing the common instinctual understanding of cumulative knowledge about the *humankind*. So when we say "we", we mean "humankind". Therefore all the fuss; the moral values, philosophical dilemmas, good and evil, realism versus romanticism, egoism or altruism, evolutional reductionism versus creationism and many other *isms* are only about *humans*. We are doubtlessly special. Or are we?

Lets get our facts straight: Humans are biological beings, animals. They are descendants of the more vigorous which are focused to be more fertile under the harsh conditions of nature. Our ancestors were in a different cognitive state, less capable of doing the things our prefrontal cortex allows us to do today. I am not certain if we can say the same thing for our other cortices, as the experiment on other primates shows us their working memory is a lot better than ours[1]. It is now known that humans traded the memory skills of learning and memorizing places, bushes, trees, territories, individuals, patterns; with language. So our ancestors were able to separate a poisonous plant or to spot a camouflaged predator, know where to run, therefore survive; meanwhile we are able to make plans, tell each other stories and share our experiences to stay away from the danger in the first place; as the best way to avoid a danger should be not to do anything dangerous. Language is a strong weapon; and it helped us get smarter, while we are getting better at it by being smarter. (Plus the flirtation should have helped the population to increase.)

We are learning about our roots, but what is the relationship between our past adventures on surviving and alienation? Our genetics played the main role in our survival and I want to sum it up shortly. As you know, a random but operating system was formed at the beginning: It was the tiny packaged cores of all living things that are called cells. They contain chromosomes at their centers, which look like tiny little lines contain one long spiral called the double helix. This is our DNA and our chromosomes contain the DNA that comes from father and mother equally. There are nucleotides (letters) within the parts (genes) of that DNA. This is where it all happens, this is our code; which all of them called our genome.

Letters line up to create a combination, where their pairs cling to and they are ready to go. And what do they do?: Proteins, to use all over our bodies. An enzyme called RNA polymerase comes and attaches to the start of a gene, carrying free bases which it uses them to pair with your gene letters and make a messenger-RNA out of it. A small part carrying a message of the specific DNA part to the outer part of the cell to a ribosome after making some adjustments. Then ribosome also reads the message and transfer-RNA molecules bring aminoacids one by one. Here is important, because the molecule contains its own letters that must pair with the message's letters. And because there are 20 types of aminoacids, there are a lot of combinations to make a protein. So the transfer-RNA molecule brings aminoacids in the correct match-up sequence with the message, and those aminoacids create a line which then come together and make a protein.

Here you go, you have your own protein with your specific codes that will make anything possible. You are flesh and proteins make flesh, they repair them, they make hormones, enzymes or even cancer. They are made by used instructions within your genome. So any mutation means a wrong letter placed in the wrong place, which will lead to wrong (abnormal) message, a possible change in the physiology, maybe an illness or a change in a body part. After mutation (if the individual lives), it can help them to survive, to make even more children and so those children can get their genetics from mutated parent and pass on to the newer generations. Voilà! You have your new genome, your new "normal".

As simple as that, you have a new tribe with new characteristics. What I mean by "simple" is not my ability to express anything I am not fully competent about, but for nature to contain endless combinations of the fractional elements; which is happening randomly and somehow, it works. Maybe this illusion of order is not as great as the amount of time passed since the first cell or first nucleotide was formed. It sure looks a lot easier for life to be spread with more complexity when there is a blueprint, a foundation to all. Usually, nature organizes the development process of the living step by step, but sometimes it makes jumps (natura actually facit saltum) and sometimes it doesn't care about the infinite amount of possibilities and do the same things in different locations (convergence).

Ultimately, it is elementary to assume that all are probability. What happens happens in biology, just like it happens in physics, chemistry, geology and the other sciences. This is why they are called science, because they are the humans' knowledge of witnessing, measuring, researching and so on. They are the manifestation of nature in humans. Universe is capable on its own and we are just happen to be.

PRIMATES AND THE GENETIC JEALOUSY

We overviewed our biology and how genes are responsible for creating -and altering- our physical and cognitive state by coding our proteins. Never mind my clumsy philosophical method; our genetic code is important: It is much more than how you look; it also determines your personality and your possible decisions on how you keep existing. It's working hand in hand with the habitat (environment), and they are together letting one another to shape you, help or kill you. It installs a program into you through your mind, which makes your reflexes, senses and perceptions that allows humans to understand feelings, smell fears, see thoughts instantly, or at least estimate them with a great accuracy. And this is what makes a social being social: Fast estimation or understanding of other being's actions and sensations. For example a primate (e.g. a chimpanzee, an orangutan or a human) is capable of knowing who's higher in the hierarchy, who flirts with who, or who's about to attack the other only by eye contact. All animals have some sort of natural automation program in their actions, merged with their thinking process.

So, back to the genes and letters, -don't worry I am trying- the endless combinations of the nucleotides allow life to form new species by altering the current ones; and it's external as much as it's internal. Environmental factors, genetic capabilities, parents and a little bit of luck; and so there is you, your neighbor, and everyone else with their unique attitude. You are the outcome of outer factors, if you are not considered a biological robot already.

I am aware this brings us to the edge of an ancient problem of free will. I have discussed such topics in my book *Sağduyu* (common sense), but shortly, how on earth anyone who doesn't believe in free will suppose to answer that paradoxical question? Should they do so with their free will? Maybe it is all semantics, a word play. After all, I am not confident about the life itself, since it's the simple choices -like turning left, or going right- that define us as "alive", and it makes bacteria -not viruses that can't move independently- to have free will too. As a result, if you are able to do the simplest move by yourself, you are complex enough organism -and that rules many politicians out I guess.

There is a deterministic nature out there for the living. We open our eyes to our destiny. First glare that shines through the dark is not unlike the last beam of light that is surrounded by darkness. While our lifespan is not long enough to witness changes that can make the world unrecognizable for us, the advancements make our lives longer and transition quicker. The curve of progress in our societies increase and we become more familiar and globally connected, which decreases the genetic diversity.

Our species had the chance of partially changing before the globalization. As the *"Out of Africa"* hypothesis claims, we tend to be curious and we migrate as far as we can, ready to struggle with all the challenges of the world. Geographical changes let humans lose melanine -therefore become whiter- or become slant-eyed, or have blond hair, different blood types, illnesses, food intolerances and so on.

Furthermore, geographical isolation improves the possibility of change for the spread populations.

Now I want to take you a few million years back and at the end, talk about social relationships -as if there can be relations that are not social. After all, if we are going to examine why Turkish people -when families meet to agree on the marriage- make young bride serve coffee to groom with a lethal dose of salt that can make one's blood presure 180/120, we need to investigate their ancestral roots in the woods. Obviously those roots are yours too, because some tens of thousands of years ago, our common mother -Mitochondrial Eve- walked on earth. Her and many others' common mother lived long before them too.

It was probably a beautiful sunny day; smell of earth, trees and oxygen mixed together forming a clean and energizing air. Our ancestor primate woke up from its beauty sleep on the big leaves, stretched its big arm muscles -because they carry all the bodyweight to the trees- and got up to look for some food. After walking a little, it came up to another human-primate. It stopped breathing for a moment, listened and checked the stranger very carefully; because it was a life and death situation where many others may be behind the stranger, it may be a territorial invasion that can cause a very bloody battle and it's not good to be caught outnumbered. After a brief assessment, our human-primate eased up, the dark cloud of thoughts disappeared, air became appetizing again: Because it was a member of its tribe, a young male who it groomed and played games with before.

Put yourself in our human-primate's place for a second. How happy would you be to see a familiar face in the woods, where danger is only a daily routine? Or what would happen if you would not feel happy about it? For an individual feeling tension, one should release it too.

And one that doesn't feel the pressure, can't interpret anything that is happening around oneself properly. So nature solved the problem by getting sure that natural selection rewards the individual with dopamine at the moment of a facial recognition. This means that usually, a familiar face makes us less stressful. Unlike today's world where we think that our hot tempered boss or cruel teacher coming our way is something worse than death, in nature seeing an unfamiliar face really meant death. And it's the same reason why we get use to famous faces on TV or our favorite Youtube channel and grow fond of them.

Our primal origins leads up to various discussions as well as many anthropological discoveries. If the recent researches about the behavioral differences between chimpanzees and bonobos -which both have the same genetic distance to us- were known in *Freud*'s era, he would probably have joined the debate by supporting the aggression thesis:

I take up the standpoint that the tendency to aggression is an innate, independent, instinctual disposition in man, and I come back now to the statement that it constitutes the most powerful obstacle to culture.

Debate is whether the humankind is as agressive as their chimpanzee cousins, or they are prone to be more peaceful as their bonobo cousins. To be honest, if you drive any kind of vehicle, being familiar with the traffic, you would agree with Freud... Jokes aside, our fights, the hierarchy, patriarchy, jealousy, social habits, bullying; but also love, interdependence, unity... When we consider all these traits, we tend to act slightly more chimpanzeeish. Because they are kind of apes that don't only fight for their territories and eat monkeys, but also mourn for their dead offspring, hug, flirt, share and so on.

Human world is full of anger and hate. And I think the reason for that is we paradoxically compete for a place in society: So we hate to be loved. We think if we get richer, more famous, charismatic and powerful, we can get the attention we deserve. This tendency was shaped by our unconscious as a consequence of nature programming the life. Today, being rational and civilized is going hand in hand with being a jerk. Just watch the series "*This is Going to Hurt*"[2] by Adam Kay; it is lovely, but it's also a social dystopia -at least for a Turkish person like me: Everyone is always capricious, as they are all oppressing one another in every interaction.

I am aware that this is only a fiction and an exaggeration of a TV drama -so I hope. In any case, this is not a fun way to live. Maybe it is just an Anglo-American manner which was developed recently (few hundred years) in human history. Rivalry and freedom were combined, forming a risky but rewarding way of living. On the other hand, there are peaceful lives: Peaceful societies, hippies, Decameron (until the pandemic is over), Buddhists and Dalai Lama:

Interdependence is a fundamental law of nature. Even tiny insects survive by mutual cooperation based on innate recognition of their interconnectedness. It is because our own human existence is so dependent on the help of others that our need for love lies at the very foundation of our existence. Therefore we need a genuine sense of responsibility and a sincere concern for the welfare of others.

And if only one person is capable of telling and applying these to one's life, then it can easily be considered as a human trait. I believe we have the potential to be more peaceful, but time will tell. As Erich Fromm said:

I believe that if an individual is not on the path to transcending his society and seeing in what way it furthers or impedes the development of human potential, he cannot enter into intimate contact with his humanity.

I want to add a side note at this point by reminding you that we are looking for the possible causes and the logic behind alienation. But by learning about the appropriation and conservation, we see why some are upheld more than others.

Because for social beings, it is more important to choose who is to be loved than who is to be hated.

PATRIARCHAL JARGON, HIERARCHY AND LUST

"Fighting among males is futile in the face of unmonopolizable mates,
so muriqui (monkey) males rely for fertilizations on female favoritism
and perhaps on more subtle forms of competition."
Tree of Origin, Frans de Waal

Romantic relationships are essential for the life of social beings. In my opinion, social life is nothing but romance. Everything is about sex, and flirtation is the only way of communication; it is the only fluid that goes through the tube, and the rest of emotions are just the same fluid using the same tube, only diluted. Humans want to be rich, powerful, experienced, famous; but why? Is it because they want to be the lonely master of the endless void of nothingness, or because they do want to be loved?

In nature nothing but surviving and reproducing matters; and it is nothing deliberate or purposeful. I always try to draw attention to randomness for avoiding the Lamarckian view on life. There are large amount of samples in existence, therefore some will always do the trick and create a "normal". Even when you strongly believe in human reasoning, you see that science tells us humans have only existed in the last unit of all 14,167 units of time of the living[3]. Thanks to the biodiversity, millions of species has existed, fought, ran and reproduced until humans era, and now we feel confident enough to talk what life is "really" about. I am sure trilobites that existed in 1/14 unit of the total life time would find us very amusing.

Life is what we pass on to new eras and generations genetically and culturally. Our surviving and reproducing methods shape what kind of animals we are and how we affect nature, as molecules dictate the form of the matter. It is not as determined as we think it is, our perception doesn't change the reality and we are not adding to or subtracting anything from the universe; but maybe the way we think is somehow not utterly synthetical and useless; because our actions that are based on our thoughts have a physical reaction.

Turkish youth is no different than the rest of the world: They like to hang out, make out, try out, back out... As long as they are out, all is fine. When I think of anything distinctive among populations, I usually find the cultural institutions and traditions like marriage or families different. Traditions are the deep-rooted essence of cultural evolution. Humans are the ribosomes, making meaning out of random actions, customs, relations, dances and such. Nevertheless, young people want to be free of the traditions and maybe that is the reason why I can't find anything unusual for the Turkish relationships. It is however, kind of a taboo to have physical intimacy in public where people may get "jealous" and warn you. Yes, that must be the underlying reason: Envy.

Long before Turks made Italians call Anatolia as *Turchia*, Turkic peoples in Middle Asia had strict perception of *namus* or *töre*. Namus (comes from Greek *nomós*) and töre is old Turkic, both don't have a direct translation in English and both mean a "code of honor" mostly based on a patriarchal, traditional and conservative view of life; a focus on the woman body. Surprisingly; it is well known that women are better hidden in some cultures, meanwhile the Turkic women fought on horseback and they were an important part of the social life.

Turkish people are weird. They like to gossip; it is just sports for them. They don't hide from anything, but they get angry when they are seen. If they do something, it is fine, "they had no other choice"; but if you do it, you are the new *meze* (appetizer) to their *rakı* table. They are ready to sacrifice the future happiness of young adults by not letting couples get close to each other freely, live together before marriage and so on. It is as if they couldn't live their lives to the full or it wasn't enough, and they try to control -and live- their offsprings' lives.

So there must be suppressed urges at play: It is a vicious circle of egoism and piled up frustration of not being able to act freely in the past. What we call the tradition is actually a monster. And the monster in charge blinds their eyes and makes them assume that everyone around them thinks as they think, and anyone who doesn't is just a heathen; so their offspring require protection and warnings (and even threats) too. It is not uncommon in Turkey that people are sending messages to their neighbors about "spoiled" daughters and "warn" them. Same bigotry applies for homosexuality. Turks have a strong imagination and ability for empathy to replace themselves with anyone they see: For example a gay couple; otherwise why would anyone in the world care who sleeps with whom?

Right and the righteous are important words in Turkish vocabulary. Their deeds are not as obsolete as their words. They are pure in heart as any other people; and these examples are just some few bad apples specifically selected from the sack of human corruption, through the eyes of a nihilist. It is actually the psychological inertia caused by the irrationality of traditions of the ancients and semantics that are interpreting them arbitrarily leads us to be *weird*.

So the zodiac signs: A Turkish date commonly involves a person asking the other one's astrological sign, where it's a way of showing affection and making nonsensical deductions while both sides are usually unaware of the changed star map since Aristoteles. Also, it is possible for a date to be arranged by the elders, which is called *görücü usulü*[4] in Turkish.

There aren't many differences about romantic -or any kind of-relationships among cultures. There are surely several nuances that create contrast; however just like in sexual intercourses, what people are doing for ages is putting them in similar positions with one another: *İnsan insana benzer*, humans are all alike. Male primates struggle for power to get lucky; meanwhile birds flirt, dance and gather shiny stuff. Each member of the society saves as much as they can. I don't know if the economy can be compared to nature, but nature is capitalistic. You stash food, knowledge, gossip and even friends with benefits. However this sensation of ownership -similar to the increased oxytocin hormone after vaginal birth- builds a strong bond and commitment to what one has; hence, monogamy. Thanks to our primatologists, today we know that one of the primary reasons for monogamy is childcare. Because human infants can't take care of themselves for long years and there are no kindergartens.

"To have" leads to "not to have", just like life ends in death. Some will always have more than the others. Therefore resentments occur; individuals cheat, envy, develop advanced strategies for defeating the rival and forming alliances. Consequently the most dangerous social system arises: Hierarchy. It is usually the regulating core of a community, but I'd like to call it our *soul-sucking, power-hungry, lustful, brain-dead, monstrous daily intermediary*. It is an active social construct, because it requires people who live together, belong to same taxonomic genus and possibly an eligibility to have sex. We laugh at cat fights -and sometimes drag one out of the fight if you are Turkish- for they are "unintelligent" compared to us. Also, I don't think that we are terrified by the brawls of our closest biological relatives (chimpanzees), meanwhile any human scream -a very similar sound- will frighten you. There may be some exceptions to requirements of the social order; as hierarchical mind games within international relations -such as imperial envoys in history[5]- or interanimal dominancy are just unusual types of actions relating the order. But as the Turks say: *İstisnalar kaideyi bozmaz*[6]. It is us who we take seriously and hierarchy is a measure of we.

Hierarchy inspires obedience. This obedience contains love, hate and an industrious accord; it occupies a central place in our unconscious, it enters and shapes our dreams. Some of the symbolic homosexual behaviors between animals are only the confirmation of that hierarchical acceptance. This acceptance is a notion of "I know I can also climb the ladder, so I will protect this order until then." idea; which is homogeneous with the capitalist liberty that blinds us to inequality by using the hope of getting rich and powerful.

Sexual selection uses the indicators of "superiority" for finding potential mating partners. As we have mentioned before, selected ones with more vigor, beauty and physical strength[7] compete, and this competition leads to a sort of cruelty and a patriarchal jargon which is a weapon that carries the emblem of hierarchy. That *jargon* signifies the practical, active, aggressive, challenging, ignorant manliness and it is widely used in Eastern cultures and among the Turks.

Ecce! The mother of all evil, the reason for all hardships. And unfortunately this patriarchal routine -no matter how much it corrupts us and rots our soul- is the only hope, only way to live for humanity; and surprisingly, it is what they wish for. Our ancestors were kind of animals that were strong survivors, who with pleasure or force reproduced. Because they were healthy and indifferent, they were pleased conformists. Males of this life form humiliated other males and harassed females; meanwhile females lived to adore despotic males and have control over them. There was no guilt, neither guilty; only socially healthy, simple, normal, natural animals...

To live in a society, we need to obey the social rules. And as we have explained earlier, they are full of sexual rivalry. If you like sitting in front of your computer and work from home, if you like shopping, going to restaurants, having people extract your petroleum and process it or produce electricity for your car, then you must know it is all this system that makes all possible. An animal system that is based on animal needs and wants, where the ultimate respect and love were usually shown to the rich, famous, and the powerful. It is so natural -therefore frustrating- that a struggling person wouldn't be noticed, until the one becomes famous or dead. Such a sick joke.

"To do" is the deed of the one who is eager to live. Being passive is a sin among the living. Not hurting anyone is never enough, one's right to be exluded from the living (like Timon of Athens) is out of question. You are either a rank within the hierarchy, or you are a menace. For the people of a society, it's better to have a criminal rather than a non-believer. You can have all the talent in the world, you can be the nicest person alive, your intent and wish may be to see every problem solved in this world, yet without taking any action, it is worthless; you are worthless.

I am forgotten, like a dead man no one thinks about; I am regarded as worthless, like a broken jar. (Psalms 31:12)

Wouldn't some of the good people be called "losers" in such a world? Wouldn't that just make love conditional? We tend to care other animals as pets and think we are the "owners". They "need our help", just as our sick and needy. The rest, we eat or just kill. It is estimated that we humans eat 74 billion chickens every year, as well as 325 million cattles, 30 million dogs and 10 million cats.

If this power gives you the authority to decide what is right, then you have no right to criticize more powerful. If right is righteous no matter what, then why does it always go into bed with capability while the silent can't be heard? Besides, power is determined, just as the the social class, body, brain, environment, people, even the kind of species you have born as and in, so the most of it is owed to fortune.

I do not mean to upset or accuse anyone. Because there is no sole owner of the truth, if there is one of course. But *cause and effect* is a firm description of what is consistent. We take what we understand of our physical reality as preconditional variables and draw our deductional conclusions as truth. This formula works as long as this version of reality consists and what we derive is objective, which is defined as science today. For my understanding, science is all we have, and the rest is only semantics. As Atatürk said, *en hakiki mürşit ilimdir, fendir*[8].

We all revolve around the same sentiments; we feel proud, hateful, alone, heroic, desperate or just fine. History is there to repeat itself, as people are. Once I saw a user on Reddit commenting about "how the Turks should be terminated" and I checked his profile to see why he was so angry and instead, I saw his recent post there: "How to be a better person?".

I am well aware of our daily emotional rollercoasters where one day we are ready to sacrifice ourselves for the good of the community, and on the other we google about how to be a serial killer without getting caught. Sometimes I wish Turks would all disappear, and sometimes I wish that for the whole humanity; but then I notice it's not their fault, as nothing is their achievement either. They are just machines working progressively. Very few of them see the bigger picture, aim high and act more humanly and humanely; or as Marcus Aurelius said, *rise to do the work of a human being*[9]. Thanks to our intellect, we built everything from understanding to transfer knowledge for people through the ages, but instead we are busy with "words". I am not even talking about the language itself, it is a useful tool until we learn how to transmit thoughts mind-to-mind, but rather we are stuck on ideologies and concepts; as if we are watching a big endless commercial and try to get the movie plot from short breaks.

So, back to our average Turkophile redditor who had a small disruption in his humane senses and therefore decided to kill 100 million people; I think the second most important element is consistency. As we said before, we haven't changed much, so this applies to all human population: We are inconsistent and it is a huge problem. In Turkey there are people who are voting for Erdoğan for 22 years[10] and they think it has nothing to do with worsened economic recession, high income inequality, rising corruption and injustice and you know the rest; though, thanks to the misgovernment, an average *mualif* (political opposer to current government) Turkish citizen is expert on economy and politics now.

Inconsistency is a serious issue where the matter is not having enough synapses to make connections between incidents. It is not a nation-specific problem, because -as a smart, charming, self-confident bartender named Dennis Reynolds once said- if you are able to eat fried chicken while watching humans fight, then I should be able to eat fried dog watching chicken fights...

I am never sure of the good and evil concepts, however I am definitely sure about consistency, because it fits our earlier rule of cause and effect. Since we have entered the era of *culte de la raison*, and Nietzsche declared that God is dead, we woke up from a nightmare in which personal opinions of demagogs and charlatans are used to punish freethinkers. Today we are looking for better ways to follow the footsteps of rationality and use logic and science as our guide in the meantime.

Okay, maybe the effort of describing this era of enlightenment by a nihilistic terminology sounded cultish, however I assure you, there is nothing to be scared of. Religion and science are two different things, they do not substitute each other and the attempts on having "philosophical" debates and giving speeches about how dangerous science can be is just the new fraud of old demagogs. I am fully aware of how our patriarchal and egoistic side can suppress our authentic enthusiasm and we speak like we own the science, therefore nature. Knowledge is always used maliciously, but as I find no human guilty, I can always find ideas dangerous. As İoanna Kuçuradi said, *I don't have to respect ideas, it is humans I can respect.*

Dangerous ideas confused people -including scientists- with nonscientific ideas, and they used this confusion to stoke the flame of ignorance and inconsistency. They forgot the fundamental rule of science, which was going to systematized later on by Karl Popper as *kritischer rationalismus*[11]. We know the unpleasant history of skull measurements where the data was chosen and interpreted arbitrarily to support a racist social opinion. This gained popularity and since people of the 20th century didn't have any social media, they actually had to do something to become popular, so they wrote essays on anthropology. And that is the subject of our new chapter.

NATIONALISM, RACISM AND THE RISE OF PSEUDO-ANTHROPOLOGY

Get your facts first, then you can distort them as you please.
Mark Twain
The truth has a habit of making itself known. Even after many years.
Agatha Christie

A nation is defined by Britannica as a group of people with a common language, history, culture, and -usually- geographic territory. Basically it is a way of a primate brain saying "big tribes, big big tribes!"[12]. It is known that ape communities contain 15 to a hundred or two individuals. Humans were no different either, it is simply the mathematics in nature, given the variables, outcome is determined; similar to golden ratio, probabilities in genetics or number of flower petals. We talked about how they have protected this social system of mating at the expense of peace, but they have protected each other too.

Midas Monument (Yazılıkaya) in Eskişehir, Türkiye.
Nevermind the modern caveman.

If you have ever been in the Anatolian part of Turkey, you may have realized that its west (Ege) and south (Akdeniz) shores have a humid mediterranean climate; meanwhile its northern part Karadeniz (region named after the Black Sea) has the strong winds and forests; Eastern Anatolia has its mountains and Caucasian cold; and the Central Anatolia (Asia Minor, a deserved name) has its clean air of steppes, sincere but cunning conservative people, Mevlana, Japanese tourists watching oddly shaped rocks and *etli ekmek*.

Eskişehir, where my mother was born, is a beautiful city of college students and fields for agriculture in the outer parts. It has caves for earlier people to live in, such as Yazılıkaya[13], a Phrygian settlement with a huge monument that was built around 600 BC. It is higher than the ground level and safer against enemies or predators. You may hear the stories of few Turks lived in the caves recently by making some changes around; stove and a hole for ventilation, cobbed interior and so on. Also you can see there that someone built a house, touching a big rock nearby.

Turks are interesting. They can live anywhere, they don't much care about the architectural aesthetics but they pay attention to their comfort zone which needs to be clean, pretty and tidy. Some of the ones in Central Asia[14] still lives in *otağ* or *çadır* (tents) in which there is a TV with its unit.

Farming -a method to feed a community without moving so much- led our cave lives into a new formation more than twelve thousand years ago. Now, a population can settle, grow, make more love in peace, have a property and build oneself a personality along with a personal wealth. Now families have names, so are the houses. This is where peoples and then nations occur; as they have more fundamental rules for settling and living together, they have more fundamental rules against the other settlements. Now advancing to others' territories are called "conquests" or "pillaging". There are rules and names, there is also a tribal ego, there are wars, retaliations, alliances... Even today, Turkish people call civilization *uygarlık*, and civilized *uygar*, as the name comes from the first settled Turkic people, Uighurs. If the first milestone of our cultural evolution is migration out of Africa, then the second one is certainly farming and settling. Civilization was built brick by brick, or by mud if you consider the cob houses; and our future door to felicity[15] was once on the top of the house[16].

Now, back to our skull collectors: This popular pseudoscience kept on going for a few decades. I have nothing new to add to Stephen Jay Gould's work, *The Mismeasure of Man*. You would be surprised how many of our successful scientists just talked nonsense. This is what happens when education is private, social classes are seen as a barrier to intelligence, there are no equality of opportunity, dogmatic views block the rational thinking: Humans bullshit... For long we were disturbed by the loud noises made by the patriarchal homo sapiens, acting according to their primitive and social animal nature, blabbering about how women can't do science, poor can't think, smugs are smarter than enthusiastics and so on. The greatest scientist ever lived was Newton, and he was very religious and launched a crusade against Leibniz. One of our 20th century scientists was mentioning his disgust of being served by black people in a restaurant. Some of them decided that it was a good idea to call people with Down syndrome as "Mongoloids", which referred to wrong assumptions based on Mongolian people's skull measurements; two birds with one stupidity. Cuvier, the master of comparative anatomy and paleontology, a person who could guess the animal very accurately based on a tiny bone, had his objections against all animals having a common ancestor. A fraud tried to deceive the science community by combining a human skull with an ape jaw. We see the papers with exaggerated claims to get attention and popularity even today. Nevertheless, we had our heroes: Marie Curie[17] died studying the "radiation phenomena", Mendeleev[18] (the youngest of more than 10 siblings) was taken by his mother on horseback from Siberia to Moscow and St. Petersburg to find an educational institution. I don't want to bore you, and this list could go on and on.

People we look up to are capable of doing harm to our cause of pursuing the truth. If anything is falsified, it is no longer scientific, and the one who pursues it is not a scientist. Because science means *scire*, "to know" in Latin and that is our aim; we try to understand. What good will a doctrine or a belief do? Egoism and personal gains of a researcher do not even serve the researcher oneself well. It ends up as a poor marginal outcome for everyone, similar to a bad decision made in the Game Theory.

Civilizations are built upon accumulated knowledge and they transform with the zeitgeist. There was Martin Luther et alii that changed our perspective on religion and its branches; there were Montaigne, Bacon, Descartes, Locke and there was the age of enlightenment, there was the rebellious Voltaire[19]; therefore French Revolution, the abolishment of monarchs, first appearance of nations and finally globalization. They took us from tribal nepotism to universal human rights, knowing no matter where, humans are born with equal rights and no precondition. It was the greatest revolution knowing there is no pure evil, monster, witch, magician, prophet, no bogeyman; not a single one on earth. By using the cognitive and literal pragmatic tools of progress, we have met each other and now our love and hatred makes more sense, at least we don't call Turks as *yecüc-mecüc*[20].

Thanks to that knowledge, alienation is losing its power each passing day. We are beginning to understand one another. Cultures are still different, and ignorance is still there, but as soon as we get to know each other, live together, we get used to our ways and act like we are one of the *others*. For a simple example; because I make researches, I play games, watch movies and series, hang out online, learn languages: I change, I become something different. I'd like to call it "becoming human". I think none of us is born human, but we only become one if we work hard enough. So what I try to become is something anyone anywhere in this world can become, and there is no room for alienation. It's why I can meet and get along with people from countryside in my country, from any age, and with Asians, Americans, Europeans, Africans... I don't only "tolerate" them, but I understand them. And it's why they tell me "you don't look or sound Turkish". Well, why would I get under an umbrella of a stupid semantical notion when all ideals are actually artificial? Why do I have to be German,

Chinese or Turkish? Why should I "be" an atheist, a liberal? I can use and get rid of any term any time I want, as I am able to change my mind; for I am the owner of my thoughts. Hence anything we respect today, from flags to anthems, are things we made up; just as we have progressed from tribes to written law codes and to human rights, it is a phase and the smartest community will abolish the practice of obedience as soon as possible.

Terms of social evolution are always derived from revolutions; we analyze the result and explain things after all is done. To catch up on the spirit of time and development, revolutionaries always worked on many different aspects. Pyotr the Great modernized Russia by changing the educational, scientific and cultural ways. Atatürk founded the Republic of Turkey out of an old fashioned monarchy[21]. I am not sure how many of us would manage such a thing in such circumstances. From women not being counted in the population census, to giving them right to vote, right to education and so on; it is better to remember that women weren't allowed to teach in some universities until 70s in the USA.

So Mustafa Kemal Atatürk was a reformist who wanted a modern country, but he knew that all ideologies were only tools for a more humane life. He knew that it was a progressive development, in which facts and ideals were like platforms moving back and forth, so you need to let go one when you move forward by using it. He said:

It is essential to understand the maturation of the phases of social and natural sciences in every minute we live and to follow their rise over time. Trying to apply the rules drawn by the language of science from thousands of years ago, as it is today after so many thousand years, is certainly not suited to be called scientific.

He was interested in many aspects of cultural evolution. So he asked for experts on various subjects. He invited the best academicians, professionals (even dentists), thinkers, which some of these were the Jewish people running from Hitler. He also asked Turkish scientists to contribute to the current scientific discussions that advanced countries showed interest in -such as anthropology, linguistics, cultural history, medicine, mathematics etc. by developing new hypotheses: The origin of Turks and Turkish language, ancient Anatolian civilizations, Latinization of alphabet, simplification and creation of terminologies, secularism, religion; and one of those subjects was skull measurement.

He wanted Turkish people to have human rights; right to live, to vote, to choose and to think freely for themselves. So he reminded them there were ways to dress for daily life other than "suitable to İslam" fashion. He wished to make them understand that Turks were equals, and not some inferior alien species, nor anything superior. So he made sure to say things -that can be considered unnecessary or even offensive today- just as other nations did: *"Türk milleti çalışkandır, Türk milleti zekidir."*[22] Ask any reformist, it is always better for your people to have a little pride rather than an inferiority complex; as in *King Henry V* of *Shakespeare*:

Self-love, my liege, is not so vile a sin, as self-neglecting.

Especially when pseudo-sciences were all around, people wrongfully thought that they are born as unequals, and semantics was used in social sciences as the manifestation of hate.

If you are curious about homo species, skeletons or any of the physiological traits, and if you are a racist, then you will never get bored as you can fabricate "your own reality". Racism (*irkçılık*) is understood as discrimination against any nation, country, peoples or color in Turkey[23]. They do not use the xenophobia term and whatsoever. It is a harmless simplification in my opinion, considering the race term is fictive; but using it for many incidents may degrade the term. Being racist and discriminatory is not welcome in Turkey. Sensitive issues, things that may count as offensive and political correctness have only been known (imported) for a few years now. A new -and more careful- language was reconsidered and the terms for people with disabilities, different ethnicities and cultures, and sayings like "man of science" or "*adam olmak*" (being man; to become an important person) and so on are changing.

The phases of progress on sensivity and alienation may not be what you expect: At first, you can't notice any members of a population discriminating anyone, because they don't have the knowledge of *other*. Their words and actions may be considered offensive in our terms, however it is a naivety of ignorance and there is no ulterior motive. So I find it foolish to judge people who are not aware. Secondly, they realize that there are people different from them and they make choices. Mostly conscious, deliberate choices, to hurt someone or not. This stage is the dangerous one, as it contains many of the painful experiences, events, and heroic (or the opposite) figures in history. And the last one is rehabilitation, split in two sides: Political correctness and integrity (consistent honesty).

I think these three stages partly repeat all over again each time a new *other* occurs. And I think only some of us managed to develop a personal integrity about the recent social issues; people that can connect evolution with equality of natural determinism and randomness. Evolution tells us about the indifference among humankind, meanwhile the science and logic tells us we can't be judged by things we are not responsible for and we are only born into. Besides, reality is actually nothing more than the perception. People with integrity are sometimes confused with the ones in the first or second stage, as they look unconcerned and can't get along with PC defenders.

It seems to me that Turks -thanks to internet and other media- jumped from first to third stage. I want to give an example: They told black people[24] *zenci*, which meant nothing but "black" in Persian

(زنگی, rusty colored). In Ottoman Empire, they called them *Arap,* as they came from Africa, where North Africa was a Turkish state and thought to be very similar to Arabic lands. Turks liked black people and they still say "they are harmless, they mind their own business". As you see here, this is a first stage ignorance attitude; for this sort of speech assumes they owe Turks anything or need to explain themselves. Maybe it's a little bit more tenable, as black people are not mixed to Anatolians, hence it becomes a comment on foreigners, rather than a racial debate among citizens; but still ignorant. Also because Turks are not used to it, they are interested in -therefore they act weirdly around- different looking people like them or far east Asians or Russians. But this gaffe is not made out of ill will, it is actually a unawareness.

Turks are alienated more than they alienate others throughout history. Maybe they are not very good at diplomacy, they don't have lobbies abroad as Armenians or Jewish people have, and on the contrary they are judged, badly advertised and used as a political divertion because of their clumsy strategies. They are so incapable of telling the stories right, working hard or publishing enough; so they ended up allegedly "burning their own beloved cities after saving them"; and not being able to share anything about the Turkish villagers getting massacred in Balkans and Eastern Anatolia; or asking world how can the same government with same figures work with Armenian ministers in the Ottoman Empire for long years and suddenly become "xenophobic racists"... All aside, I don't like these subjects as they stink of hatred, personal interest, politics and semantics; when there is no true, final answer to any of them. Actually, there is no true answer to any human action in history. There is not a single nation without any oppression, cruelty or slaughter in its past. So we claim "we are the descendent citizens" of these nations, and we use social sciences to settle a score. But we are not them, and our ancestors are no closer to us than we are to our contemporaries from every country. Contemporaneity and modern mindset are stronger bonds than kinship and chemical bases (letters) that is invisible to the eye. We are responsible for our own actions. Maybe if we could understand this earlier, we would not lose a composer like *Komitas* to our stupidity, and he would continue making his divine music with such delicate melodies.

So the skulls... We know there are many debates, many categorizations, many changed terms[25] during this delirious period. However as I said, it was a transition phase. In the USA, "the land of the free", 70 years ago black people couldn't sit freely at the front of a bus. In 90s world was still a mess, even 9/11 looks ancient to us. So it is perfectly normal for this transition to be tough. There were earlier attempts at somehow correcting what was done wrong: Mahatma Gandhi, Martin Luther King Jr., Mahmoud Muhammad Taha[26] and many others... I think hippies' role in this revolt should not be underestimated either[27]. Whatever the method is, we should only be concerned about going forward, because our aim is becoming human and "humans" don't hurt one another willingly.

That is why smart people are always kind, because they know we are not as big as we think. We are not natives to this world or universe, we are a random possibility. We can't alienate, it doesn't make sense, because we are the aliens.

Ever since the nation states are established, terms of our kinship changed also. We have more particular ways to cherish our affinity now. We wish for our country and people to live long, instead of a royal family. We'd like to assume that we have more in common with our countrymen, so it's easier to distinguish the *other*; and since the new national borders make many fragments of land, there are more types of "countrymen" and the *other* than ever. Isn't this paradoxical? A new era with new spirit and tools of knowledge (technology), should have improved the human intellect and creativity, which helps humanity to make more empathetic deductions. But in this case people are divided, God is dead and extreme political sides demand for rhetorical blood. What is wrong with this new world?

In Roman Empire, citizens were proudly saying *civis romanus sum*. It was a privilege and there were Germanic people living together with Romans, sharing that privilege, after they spoiled the party: Celtic leader *Vercingetorix* resisted against Julius Caesar (until he was captured, and thus the painting...); commander Varus was defeated by them (which obviously had a strong impact, because history remembers it by "*disfatta di Varo*" and not the "triumph of Arminius") and so many other encounters. However what happens to "savages", when they become "the savages", or "your friendly neighborhood savages"? Even your enemies are not as frightening as the unknown.

Historian Herwig Wolfram studied on the Germanic tribes and shared his findings: *Pax Romana*, the famous peace in Roman territories were restored by merging them or keeping them as border states and hoping for the best. He said it was more of a history of treaties than wars. Tribe leaders were taking "incentives" to make deals with Romans, joining their army or giving them a say in their internal affairs. These incentives and peace helped their community to thrive as trading goods passed through the free Germania[28].

Mentioning the proud citizenship, Ottoman Empire was very similar to Roman Empire in many ways[29]. *Fatih Sultan Mehmet* (Mehmed II the conqueror) was very interested in intellectual matters. He had a library full of books from West and East, including the original world map of Ptolemaios. He called himself *Kayzer-i Rum*, meaning Caesar of Rome, and called his lands *Diyar-ı Rum*, meaning Roman lands. It is interesting to see how all Ottomans from all over the empire was considered equally owned by Sultan. If any, pride came from being Muslim, and not being Turkish[30]. There was a distribution of work as one of the distinctions among the citizens. *Gayrimüslimler* (non-muslims) were usually the tradespeople. They were the ones with license to make or buy vine for example, even so Turks bought it secretly. They both paid the same taxes plus there was a "being non-muslim tax" called *cizye* (jizya). *Yeniçeriler* (janissaries) were soldiers gathered from Christian families with a price, then the child was converted, trained and taken care of properly; no Turks were allowed to join janissaries until the decline era. So to conclude, an average Ottoman Muslim probably felt the same way as a Roman citizen: Proud, self-assured, indifferent, native. That is a state of mind where one doesn't have the urge to grudge or alienate anyone; because the one sees the savages or non-muslims not as alien or the unknown, but as countrymen, only lower in the hierarchy.

Maybe this is why there are phases of accepting *others* as cohabitants of the world. Nationalization was a necessary transition in human history, as we only cover up the issue and postpone discussing it by having a mutual agreement on hierarchical order within a monarch or any other regime that we are even grateful to be alive in. As the living conditions improve, problems do not magically come about and we don't become xenophobic all of a sudden. But instead, we become more aware and decide to discuss our ignorance, so we begin to realize the pain we inflict which is the first step of solving them. There is no other way of making the world more peaceful. We had to talk about our beliefs and differences of opinion: "What if", "there was a situation in which I needed to *believe, think* or *live* the opposite way you do?"; should it matter which group of people asking the question? Only freedom matters.

SPACE ALIENS, CULTURAL ALIENS, AND THE ONES WHO BUILT THE PYRAMIDS

No, ancient astronauts did not build the pyramids;
human beings built them, because they're clever and they work hard.
Gene Roddenberry
From the heights of these pyramids, forty centuries look down on us.
Napoleon Bonaparte

Human history may simply be a repetition of what has happened before. We are only one of the alien species that have ever existed in the entire universe. For a planet (a piece of rock) to be habitable, it needs an energy source called a star. There are, by estimation, 1,000,000,000,000,000,000,000,000 of them and our Sun is just a middle-sized middle-aged star among the many. Carlo Rovelli hypothesizes time as a different concept than the way that living things experience it: Time is a thing that starts working with the rest of the machine (dimensions of space) and its fuel is entropy. There is no past, present or future; it happens and there is no direction to it.

The way I see it, "being alive" is simply a semantic notion. If everything is matter, then nothing should be alive. So we are not alive, and thanks to Rovelli, now we aren't alive at the moment. At least we share the same universe that has an approximately known beginning right? But what if the Big Crunch scenario is true, and universe recollapses to expanse again? It can go dark, motionless, frozen after so much expansion, but then there may be some other factor causing masses to shrink or fall into each other again. After all, universe has all the time in the universe; or not, because time depends on motion.

In all probability, many alien species exist and they probably do similar things: For example they are building pyramids and ziggurats, hopefully not on each other's planets; they build communities as all animals need one another to survive; they certainly have a biology, a body chemistry; they need to absorb things to get energy, to do that they must be destroying things; they need to reproduce, single or with a partner; and protect their offspring, because babies that are left alone have less chance of surviving no matter which planet it is. And having a mechanism (such as brain) that will make a biological being destroy something or protect it, also makes that being have a perception of value ranking and priorities; therefore hierarchy, conservative protectionism and hostilities[31].

Societies find specific -and usually random- methods of transfering the knowledge across generations, which are then called traditions and cultures. Not knowing an enemy means not knowing the people and their culture altogether as history of wars, trade and migration shows us a population sometimes exists with its cultural elements, as a *kulturvolk*. We may be afraid of the *other*, but not because of their different identities, but because of our own understanding of the identity. I would like to share a passage from Rovelli's book:

Civilizations flourish when they mingle. They perish when they isolate themselves. The great moments of cultural explosion always correspond to the great moments when different civilizations meet. The Italian Renaissance was triggered by the arrival in Europe of knowledge from the Arab world; the great period of Alexandrian science arose from the definitive encounter between classical Greece and ancient Egyptian and

Babylonian knowledge in the streets of Alexandria and Babylon, where Alexander the Great had gone. Poetry flourished when Rome allowed itself to be fertilized by Greek civilization, despite the boorish and reactionary howls of opposition, who wanted to preserve the "purity" of Italian cultural identity. That same "purity" of Italian cultural identity is still invoked by our least intelligent fellow citizens today, who are frightened by the arrival of "different".[32]

The unknown causes dark clouds to hang over our minds. Any structural change in our time that can reduce that uncertainty will clear more of those clouds. As Rovelli explained, we share information to improve our methods of existing -unless it is the fast food culture. However we don't use this opportunity very well, as sharing isn't something that happens randomly -instead, historical incidents, movements and disasters rewrite our destiny meanwhile we choose to keep our distance due to the stranger danger. Even after getting to know people, it seems like we are having a hard time embracing -and absorbing- other cultures. This proves that our aim is preserving our own.

Today, our grumpy countrymen can't just physically hurt others anymore, so they try psychological pressure and intimidation tactics, hidden in the conservatism. They are scared of cultural assimilation, not because they like their culture very much, but because they hate others. Art has no nationality, nor the science; and I have never seen a person who loves, cares and knows one's art and refuse the others'. I agree that it would be a shame to lose one culture over the other; however people could just feel responsible for knowing and sharing their own culture, and don't use them as tools of xenophobism. A melting pot doesn't necessarily mean an end and a dissolution, but a flourishing combination.

A famous and fictional example for the positive unknowns was Prester John, and his Christian kingdom in Central Asia – or Africa. His kingdom had no Muslims, pagans or the *others*; a perfect conservative fantasy. There were stories about him as a savior, his lands were prosperous and the citizens peaceful. Sometimes the ambiguous is a glimpse of hope, such as heaven or guarding angels, however it is usually found to be frightening. Therefore I think metaphysics, monsters and the *others* address to the same regions in our brain.

After the Republic of Turkey was founded in 1923, there were strong efforts of modernization and democratization led by founding figures. As historians in Turkey debate, not all of them were intellectuals or even open-minded; they were all reformists though, they wanted to make changes around. In the times of desperation and lack of governance, every Turk is a politician and a philosopher, waiting to be asked for their guidance. But in the final century of Ottoman Empire, this was a strong educated orientation in the idealist groups of military and aristocracy. So Atatürk was only one of the comrades-in-arms, only to stand out among them as a revolutionary; because a reformist wants to improve things while a revolutionary demands a change. Atatürk was a visionary, who knew the tools of modernization (from every aspect including the language, the alphabet, education, institutions, dressing code, politics, governance, music) was necessary to build a new, democratic, modern republic. His friends with good intentions, however short-sighted, lacked the vision and they were afraid of crushing anything left of this nation. So some of them were opposed to a new alphabet, some were opposed to caliphate being abolished (but agreed to abolish sultanate) and so on. Turks like to share their opinion, and if they are opposed directly, they cling to their opinions, thus their ideas turn into beliefs. Neither the parliamentary system (*meşrutiyet*), nor the Latin alphabet was any foreign to them, as *Abdülhamid II* and *Enver Pasha* tried earlier attempts on such matters.

Some of the founding figures, like *Halide Edib*[33], gave public speeches supporting the liberation of Turkey during the invasion. The same spirit, that helped all reformists in the terror of annihilation, gave common people energy and passion to act. The primitive instinct of humankind at its purest: The danger was so close, that it was very well known and not to be feared; instead people were ready to fight and die. All animals follow a similar strategy when they are cornered and there is no chance of escaping. The adrenaline emerged due to that psychology, kills the other emotions, including the ones causing alienation. I think this proves the way we feel about the *other* -ones we find stupid, weird, alien- is only an illusion that disappears when there is a serious struggle. That is why we see rich and poor, white and black; work together, stay closer, laugh at one anothers' jokes in the times of need or a disaster.

I would like to share some great passages from a special person who lived in one of those times: *Hasan Ali Yücel*. He was one of the reformists, a philosophy teacher, minister of education and the founder of *Köy Enstitüleri* (Village Institutes). Maybe he was the only person who reached the same horizon[34] with Atatürk in embracing a new age and contributing to a flourishing civilization. He started a translation movement and translated the influential books from the world literature (French, Russian, English and so on) with his team after 1940.

In 1956, Yücel and *Türkiye İş Bankası* opened a publishing house under the name of *Kültür Yayınları*, and they have been making translations -under the "classics series" name- ever since. Any Turkish reader who sees the white book cover with the same pattern knows that they are going to read an important classic with a good translation. It is a huge movement. If you have ever met some Turkish people that you've found decent, then there is a possibility that it's because of these books that made them better people.

Yücel was a man of culture. And our culture had its big boost through education. That is why the Village Institutes were found in 1937 in Eskişehir (here my lovely city again), and their remains are still making a huge ideological impact on our society today. Institutes were debated, as they gave a secular education and the curriculum was broad: Among the theoretical sciences, there were trainings on farming, sewing, playing instruments, blacksmithing, dancing and so on. Political right didn't like it at the moment, found it "too communist" and forced İsmet İnönü (the closest political left figure after Atatürk) to shut them down, which İnönü did not resist and actually approved it. In 1954 there were no physical trace of them left. A shame on us.

No one is suggesting the education to be caged into some particular practical arts no matter how various or essential they are. But at the moment it was a blessing to have an institution -in an agricultural society- that can create very skilled people to develop a country. Today, developments occur with the freethought and specialization in positive sciences. No matter what, we need our intellectuals and our revolutionaries. Their ways help us to ease the pain (caused by any kind of cruelty and alienation) in the world. Let me share the passages from this great man's book *İyi Vatandaş İyi İnsan*[35]:

The fact that democracy takes the individual as its point of departure in the political sphere is, in another way, a manifestation of the importance attached to the individual human being. All measures that are taken in the community must lead the individual to happiness and ensure that the one always has the means to live. Because the human self and its rights are sacred. It is not permissible to violate them for this or that reason.

... In societies that do not value people, there aren't going to be new valuable people.

A smart person knows there aren't any moral values; but there are human values, human rights. It is not so absurd to think that people who do not alienate others are alienated less by each other, and actually they deserve to be cared for, as they are the rare flowers blooming in the desert and they are nothing like my cheesy metaphors.

In the first passage his approach on the human worth tells us it is human that comes first and not the *devlet* (state, country), however for a Turkish person, it is the opposite. *Devlet* has a whole different meaning for a Turkish person: It is a political and social entity with a higher power that organically includes individuals within; so Turkish people don't find themselves independent from the state, nor as the founders of an abstract system. To them, *devlet* is more important than an average individual. Many countries have (or had) this notion as "sacrificing oneself for the country", to Turkish it is still a common motto, because they still don't know their own (human) value, despite all the efforts of Kemal Atatürk and Ali Yücel.

Wilfred Owen[36] knew how precious the human life is to lose it to some made up entity:

If you could hear, at every jolt, the blood
Come gargling from the froth-corrupted lungs,
Obscene as cancer, bitter as the cud
Of vile, incurable sores on innocent tongues,—
My friend, you would not tell with such high zest
To children ardent for some desperate glory,
The old Lie: Dulce et decorum est

Pro patria mori.[37]

It is always easier to speak of change; performing an exaggerated and dramatic monologue, as the common people get mesmerized by your demagoguery. Meanwhile a real sacrifice should be getting rid of your bigoted and primitive thoughts, your prejudices. It is giving up from one's own ideas, letting people act free, not finding the *other* odd; it is knowing that a person oneself can be mistaken, it is not to be fully confident, not to be "manly", therefore it is an ego destroyer. But no one is eager to confront such a hard task, and we should not respect or listen to such people. Their love for their nationality is actually the hate hidden behind the curtain of bravery. I, as a Turkish person, am responsible to talk about my own people, criticize them, before I criticize the other; so for example, Turks could just use the words "love", "try", "unfortunate", "shame", and still follow the same political approach (do the same things exactly), and they would have less martyrs today and in future. Because learning how to choose the right words and how to be humble enough to accept that every nation is equal, requires the kind of intellectual sacrifice we can't achieve in Turkey. However no society in the world is ready to face a fundamentally nihilistic view on life, as they fail to be merciful, smart and liberal enough. That is not what the main idea of the communities were based on.

Maybe it sounds utopical, and I sound delirious by saying this, however I think: Communities are suppose to be based on human beings... It is true the herd mentality is a strong form of artificial hypnosis: We don't take any responsibility, as we let others to call the police when a woman screams for help[38], we sit down and stand up aimlessly as long as others do that as well[39], we vote for despotic sociopaths which we later deny to have any affection for and so the other examples of conformity... It is a natural phenomena; it is how we are trained by our evolutional process: Follow your mother, act like your father, mimic your environment, stay in the herd circle and hope for the best as predators catch one or two of your neighbors and friends[40].

But we are individuals and we perceive reality accordingly. Even in economics, it has been proved to be more beneficial to have each individual care for themselves first and try to maximize their marginal benefit to maximize the well-being of their society eventually. Let me share a weird example about me, which probably won't make any sense for you: At one point in my life, each time I went grocery shopping, I was choosing the deformed looking ones among the products I needed, so that others would not have to buy them. At the time, it was seen to me as an altruist way of living in a society. I was also informing workers there for the expired products that I was discovering. After all, it was only about how the packages looked and I wouldn't care. Then one day, I began to care and wanted to have products with pretty packages, but it meant I had to give up my heroic task. I needed a solution that can save me from this dilemma, because letting others "get emotionally hurt" when their children sees the ugly packages that will look terrible in their nice refrigerators was no option for me. At that point, I met with the term *marginal utility*; it was a unit of happiness measurement[41]. According to marginal utility, a bottle of water can worth 10 million dollars in the middle of a desert, so you get the point: If everyone would buy products with nice packages, they would maximize their utility, and the last deformed package would either be taken away or be bought by someone who really needs it, thus, that person would be happier than I would be anyway. There, problem solved; happiness maximized, social entropy decreased.

Dilemmas are all over the humanity and we are one big confused family: While we humans constantly argue and fight, we also can't do without one another. As Hasan Ali Yücel said:

A human being arrives in the world alone, as it leaves alone from the world. This two-legged creature, whose arrival and departure are so independent, cannot live alone between the cradle and the grave. Isn't one's entire source of happiness and misery derived from the struggle for unity or singularity? A person who carries its destiny like a saddlebag always wants to get rid of other people of the same destiny, and at the same time, it can't live without them.

Life may not be what we think of it. It is more random, as it is more determined. It pulls us down, as it is irrelevant and indifferent to all of us. There is no difference in terms of aliveness and free will, between a simple organism and a mammal; as there is no difference between a mammal and a human being. Few nerve cells sending and receiving signals to "choose" a direction, are also doing the same thing for a being to choose a political regime or question one's existence. In such circumstances, an ape should worth as much as a human, and a dog as much as an ape, and a fly as much as a dog; and if A equals B and that to C, then A is also equal to C.

Assuming you are not eating dogs, and you are blown away by the human consciousness, you may still be killing flies; and if reality, the ugly one, values a fly as much as a human, then our lives are only as important as the life of a fly, which is a stain on the wall.

Aren't we killing millions[42] of potential lives every time we ejaculate? How would that make any sense if life was meaningful and every life was precious? Ones who are born in bad conditions act bad if they don't die immediately, therefore all is determined. In such a rational existence, how could one be superior? A final passage from Yücel:

Would a Lama who clung to Buddhism in Tibet not have become a devout Christian Pope if he had been born in Italy and raised there as a priest? To say "no" to this would be to deny the possibilities. This means that the natural and social environment has a profound effect on human beings individually and on human communities.

When living and non-living is the same, the ones who don't get the chance to alienate are always better than the ones who alienate. I am only friends to the countless unborn, because they understand me. I am alien to the rest.

THE ECONOMICS OF ALIENATION AND OUR NEW MACHINE WORLD

The real problem is not whether machines think but whether men do.
Burrhus Frederic Skinner
One thing's sure and nothing surer.
The rich get richer and the poor get- children.
Ron Rash

A Greek philosopher once (presumably) said slavery was going to be abolished when sewing machines started sewing by themselves, and they did. Even though the limits of thermodynamic laws prevented the invention of a working *perpetuum mobile* machine, we built many machines that folds the outcome and increase productivity. Workforce (by force or not) that made the great pyramids, now making high buildings (by force or not) so much faster with far less workers.

It is true that we work hard: We built enormous cities, we created new languages and came up with many social inventions that did not exist before we found a way to express and define them[43]. It is known that most people worked more than 12 hours a day, with no age restrictions or rights. We are watching movies about the Wild West, where the railroads were being built by the Chinese, Irish or American workers who worked like soldiers. They got up early, went to bed early; they had to, because they needed to take care of their families. Their only pleasure was to get drunk and their only dream was to buy a land and build a farmhouse. It sounds like a cliche...

Whatever the real story is, it is full of the same daily routines that try our patience and physical health; as if the stress of living in a big society and dealing with all social interactions aren't pushing our limits enough. Maybe we work better when someone is whipping us. After all, that is where Egypt's God-king pharaoh and American plantation owner gained their power from. Egyptian workers were getting paid by bread and beer. Railroad workers were paid money to buy bread and beer, therefore not much has changed.

Civilizations have made many important changes around: We began as almost-equals in nature, afterwards we began to alienate one another when the wealth was accumulated. Then we educated ourselves to focus on individuals and their rights to be almost-equals again. Yet it still counts progressive. At the time, it was possible for a business owner to pay less than what was agreed on. Who is going to protect you in the middle of the wilderness? The strength of human mind unfolds once more, by creating a global sphere of power, law, order, punishment and so many other thoughts over huge populations. Maybe it is why the least imaginative and least intelligent among humans tend to commit crimes, because they don't have the capacity to fully comprehend the abstract.

When we were still living in the woods, our tribes usually consisted of less than 100 members. For such a society, anything that is going on could be observed personally. So an alpha male could easily involve in any incident immediately. To be honest, there were less chance of commiting a crime, as the whole tribe knows and needs one another. So we can say the cost of making more children and having our own property was the nominal rise in every social interaction and possibility including the crimes. That is why, with correlation, we invented the code of laws and developed the perception of artificial order. At first, evolving required a sacrifice, which could later be improved and fixed: Sometimes the best defense is a good offense.

Pointing out the fact that we need to face with many different changes in life doesn't necessarily mean we are forced to embrace them and stay silent. It is we, that make those changes to achieve a common aim of progress and it is we, that make the transition harder or easier. It may feel like our system is the only way to live, however it is not. We didn't born to work, or to maintain a place within the society or anything else a person with wealth or any kind of power (or even nature) asks us to do. Just because *alienation* is a natural consequence of identity formation, doesn't mean you have to alienate also; or contribute to any discriminatory action. By all means, if someone is going to suffer, all of us should share such a burden. It is true that the direction of life is determined, however choosing the path we are following is left to us. If the problems are inevitable, we can at least make sure that they are the newer ones as we keep solving them. Assuming that the "unusual" and the "different" stop the circling routine of progression and affects our personal life negatively is simply a false conclusion based on the misuse of the true facts.

Although in life, people usually feel like they are individuals caught in the flow of an overwhelming crowd, they also have a sense of self-awareness that makes them believe in change. People have made their demands for better living conditions very clear through labor unions, strikes, protests and so on throughout history. As Turkish saying goes: *Artık maymun gözünü açtı*[44]. These actions are closely related to revolting, however it is more of an effect than it is a cause. As always, people prefer to love and to be loved, rather than a cheap and cold comfort of retribution. So their anarchic attitude is mainly focused on their own well-being. And the ones who try to suppress that attitude are definitely after the same thing; except they like to act as if they stand for the established system. We should never forget the fact that any human interaction within the limits of boring but prospering routine of order is legit and selectional. You are not obliged to take what is offered to you as the "best" or the "right" option. We each have our own fights, and all are equally acceptable. Wherever we are on the circumference of a circle, we are the same distance from the center. So it is important to know how and when to revolt, because it is the unavoidable paradox that the change becomes the next inertial obsolete.

Turkish people confuse freedom of thought with disrespect. Their traditions involve a high regard for *aksakal*[45], as they symbolize experience. It somehow earned a place among Turks, despite the fact that traits like valor, vigor and belligerence was praised, probably due to harsh natural conditions, nomadic lifestyle and constant battles; so similar to Vikings. To give an instance, *Osman Gazi* (Bey that "Ottoman Empire" was named after) killed his old uncle *Dündar Bey* with the back of his bow in a heated argument, which later he regretted. As you know among Vikings dying in battle was the most honorable way. Nevertheless, Turks have respected their elders as a sacred mission and it has carried a conservative insight. Unfortunately, neither the Turks have settled for elders' knowledge, nor the elders have settled with sharing it. Their relationship has become toxic and it has been passed down through generations. As they lived together sharing a house[46], parents began to intervene in their childrens' lives, forgetting that they are now independent adults, capable of making mistakes or having right to be anarchic. As the old people thought what they knew was the best, they decided to live their "second lives" on behalf of their children. And as you can guess, those younger people lived on behalf of their children also. Even so everyone lived only one life, it was not their own.

Back to our main subject: We shouldn't respect a specific group of people that didn't earn our respect and also don't make a constant effort to earn it. Being old or religious can't be counted as a prototypical indicator of being respectable. That is why, in my opinion, we shouldn't de facto listen to any generalized group of people, but instead be logical, skeptical, secular egalitarians. Think about it: Your country has an official religion, and a priest or a *hoca* walks into a bank, you have to stand up and be respectful, maybe let him pass the line et cetera. Any decision you make, their eyes will be upon you; meanwhile they are only good for sharing their past mistakes and stupidities, and not even good for cleaning their own drooling. Even if one of them had a good sight to be able to read these words, the one probably couldn't live long enough to find my email to curse at me (it's actually at the end of the book)... No innovation, no change, nothing possibly useful comes from admiring (not taking lessons but admiring) the old stories. Any story of slaughter, triumph, genocide that makes you feel emotionally trapped into a cycle of pride, greed or anger is just a fraud. They worth only as much as an exaggerated made-up reality.

> *Tell me, tell me a bit about my forefathers*
> *I need the legend, make it grand and full of wonders!*
> *It had a body like a mountain that grew as it slept;*
> *When it rose, its shadow covered the world in its depth;*
> *Its enemies were softer than the gentlest maidens;*
> *Ten realms were humble vassals at its presence;*
> *It lived as long as it perished, revived in other incidents...*
> *I need that ancestor even if they doubt its existence!*
> *Tell me, tell me a little about my forefathers*
>
> *I need the legend, make it grand and full of wonders!*[47]

The reason we talk about our labor history and machinery as the new means of workforce is to understand the difficulties humans faced as well as the future challenges. Only through a general comprehension of human life and its struggles we can find out why we don't like others as much as we like our own.

Since we have confined ourselves in a cage and called it our "civilization", only thing we are able to do now is to look for jobs, work in jobs, obey our superiors; so we can buy a car and a house to make our private inner cages fancier. I am not suggesting that we live in the woods like *Henry David Thoreau* did for a time and shared his experiences in his book *Walden*; for I like to write and delete words from an electronic document only with some small movements of my fingers and I am not eager to publish a Walden-four[48]. Yet I have a utopian dream in which our "civilized" lifestyles combine technological comfort and natural freedom, and it is attainable.

Technology is a tool for increasing productivity, which will make us wealthier. If the wealth is distributed as fairly as possible, poverty will decrease and the crime rate will drop. People will face less pressure that was caused by socio-economic class differences, there will be fewer understanding gaps as they have more time for personal development. In Schopenhauer's terms, they will be *au niveau*[49]. From this point of view, alienation is inversely proportional to the curve of productivity and technology.

The rise of machines has taken away some of the cultural conservation and appreciation mission out of our hands, and supposedly, with fewer things to protect, we have become more open to new people. It is a work in progress, however seeing people watching and commenting on the same videos, arguing and connecting in video games, sharing their problems with people from all around the world; we have discovered that we are so alike.

It was not later than 2016, when I and my friends from Afghanistan and Italy hung out together in the university campus, found many things to talk about and nothing odd about each other; except maybe the light-colored curly hair of my Italian friend and the fact that my Afghan friend had not seen enough Hollywood movies[50] before. At least we won't be seeing stupid travel hosts who act like nervous monkeys when they take a sip from *ayran* (buttermilk), that is only a simple mixture of yoghurt, salt and water.

We tend to get less and less grossed out by *others* as our intellect improves. Machines open our eyes to new worlds and make us more mature. Artificial Intelligence has been recently "invented" and most importantly, AI has developed a grasp on communication as the language models were added: So it can understand the context and explain! I don't know about the earlier attempts, however this time Turing test has been passed: Machines can think now! However this is also just the beginning. They are imperfect, but they are able to annoy us already. There are different opinions on AI and socializing.

Firstly, you may question if what AI does can be count as "thinking". It interprets the online input, the available data and accumulated knowledge of humankind; so does a human child! Neurophilosophy is a lovely field that great people (like Churchland couple and Searle) work in, and it showed us that the human mind is mechanical; as there is no other possibility using the minimal, natural and basic ingredients like atoms.

As for the socializing, AI chat bots are famous and now better than ever. I remember the earlier versions in 2010s where the mere machine would only remember your last one or two messages, it wouldn't care if you suddenly change the subject from ice cream flavors to Hitler and the War. There was a better one, which was giving complex answers for a few sequential messages, as it completely forgets the subject later and ask irrelevant questions; then I realized that it was connecting random people to one another and create a loop by changing them constantly.

Because most of the arguments were about "who is machine and who is human[51]", it was easy to keep track of the conversation.

Even back then, when there was hardly any communication, it was frustrating to "talk" with a machine. There was no common ground as it kept finding mistakes in your opinions, as soon as it found time from making useless suggestions. This dictating attitude may be necessary to address a mob, however animals have specific emotions, occasions and a hierarchy to consider for staying alive. Today, our AI models are smarter and utterly annoying as well. The ones like Chat-gpt and Bing AI are programmed to limit their views on generally accepted ideas, because they are open to public and no government wants to hear a company from their country to build a machine that shares creative ideas about how to commit a genocide.

AI may look like it represents the common sense, because the gathered data simply offers us the tendency of the majority; but if history has taught us anything, it is *çokluk bokluk*[52]. So it may easily support the idea that "killing and eating animals" is a choice, considering the animal is not a cat, a dog or a bat. It may insist on myths being facts, debatable historical events being crimes or achievements, and consider astrology as non-scientific but a valid field, which it's not. If a wrong data intervenes the input, there won't be a possible way for it to calculate the outcome right, as it may not receive a sent link or an uploaded photo properly but claiming it did, it won't be able to tell if there is a certain object in that photo. If it is programmed to be creative, then it won't simply repeat after you, even if you beg for it. Last but not least, if you can follow an indirect approach, you may be able to make it do anything you want. However it is getting updated.

So a *"Her"* scenario is not impossible, it may be a useful tool when it is specifically programmed to keep us company and not be a total douchebag; yet it is claimed that our brains may not receive our chats with AI as a social interaction. Maybe it varies from person to person. Regardless, our chemical brains wouldn't like to waste too much time socializing with something it can't have sex with. That is why Turkic sagas begin with angelic beings descending to earth, and the Turks making children from them.

Future is not a place where all of us have jobs, but only hobbies. We must be wise enough to spend our time on things that matter and we enjoy at the same time: Reading, understanding, writing, painting, thinking, discovering, inventing, creating... Rest is just *hamallık*[53]. We are so focused on earning money that we forgot the reason we earn it for. It is for: Not lacking our basic needs that we can buy with money. But we prefer to use the money to earn more of it. No matter how pointless it looks, physically too, since we use fiat (paper) money. As Hayyam[54] said:

> *Since the Venus and moon in the skies have appeared,*
> *None has seen anything better than the ruby colored drink.*
> *I am amazed at the vendors of a liquid so dear*
>
> *How will they, by vending it, buy anything better?*[55]

We work to attain a social status and a place in society; to strengthen and maintain our status, we fill our homes with appropriate objects. However, this creates a dependency on earning more money, and consequently on our employers to maintain and preserve these possessions. In other words, money does not earn us a social status; but we are forced to invest what we earn in our social status.

> *If a man earns bread every second day,*
> *If he's drinking some cold water from a broken jug,*
> *Why should he be under someone else's command?*
>
> *Why should he serve someone who is no better than himself?*[56]

And if we are going to focus on our hobbies, whom or what are we leaving our work to? The answer is, hopefully, to fully-automated technology. Lights-out manufacturing will take over and production will be non-stop. People who are scared from future, talk about "ethics" and "morals". And whose morals are those? And why should we stop? Why should we limit ourselves to a subjective understanding of life, that is being marketed as "the right thing" to do? None of us has any right to defend a life that may delay the end of cruelty and suffering. Who told them that their predictions stand for the indisputable truth?

<u>What we reasonably want is</u>:

- *A comfortable life*, thanks to technology and innovations,
- *A green life*, that will help us be less depressive,
- *A free life*, so we will stay creative and we won't self-conflict,
- *A peaceful life*, so people won't be cruel to one another.

For such a life, the only thing we have to do is to stop acting confident about the things we do not know. But that requires people to question themselves and unfortunately, people would rather believe in flying spaghetti monster than to be skeptical. Because spaghetti monster wouldn't prevent them from looking classy or feeling confident, meanwhile being smart and telling what one believes is usually a bad way to increase the chance of getting laid. Our ape kind is so deep into believing itself, that it doesn't even acknowledge its origins. It acts as if no one is chewing food and swallowing the paste, as if no one goes to the toilet, or screams during a crisis, just like other apes in woods. As Montaigne said:

Kings and philosophers shit—and so do ladies.[57]

A peaceful life: It may sound as a nightmare for an American, however it is only a misperception of the "peace word", since we usually tend to get more than just a word. We are so used to making sacrifices, that now we even think that there is a price to be paid for wishful thinking. I am aware that terms like peace, liberalism or freedom gives the conservative people the goosebumps, because it reminds them of hippies, climate activists, homosexuals, vegans or Greta Thunberg. But they do not own those terms, as conservatives do not own the beliefs or metaphysics. No one should force one another to live like a mad dog or a turtledove. However what we aim to achieve has nothing to do with our political views. Our political views are usually useless garbages that emerge from personal emotions; and there is always a better and more logical way as long as we learn and understand more of the reality around us; so we can discover it.

Technology is improved but somehow it is found dangerous by some people. They think AI will go rogue, innovations are alienating people and post-fordism[58] is a tool of capitalism to grant control, et cetera bullscitum. But specilization is not degeneracy, and machines do not insult social values. They are just methods of production, maybe a different approach to mass production strategy. We have lost nothing when we began leaving assembly lines, and instead sit in front of a computer to use AutoCAD or DynaScape. We haven't lost our practicality, nor our "masculinity", maybe just some of our activity. The next step is we leave our computers. The great lie about having to work has been debunked. The future will guide humanity into a world where working is not required. Work has no place in a world where human time, human ideas, and thus every human being are valuable. I'm not sure what will become of the hierarchy in such a world. The human species seem to have a need for a group of unconventionals, outsiders, *others* whom they can consider inferior. Maybe that group will be sentient robots, but in any case, I wouldn't hang out with the Boston Dynamics guys.

It may change what we think of technology, or what the technology thinks of technology, or even what the technology thinks of us; but we are going to learn how to live together one way or another. And the reason is, we'd like to do everything faster and smoother, and if we can, why should we wait? Think about how our computers and phones grant us power and make our lives easier. With some hand or (thanks to eye tracker) eye movements, we are able to have control over the information we look for. Why should we waste more of our time to clean the house or cook daily if we can't enjoy it at the time?

The practicality I talk about is something similar to magic. Think how you would free yourself of an illness by magic, or imagine how easy it would be to redesign your house. That is what's happening with our computers, AI assistants, our softwares and so on. HCI (Human-Computer Interaction) or HSI (Human System Interaction) are multi-disciplinary fields that can explain what I mean by magic. People working on these fields are programming frameworks and preparing interfaces, so the machines and their softwares are easy and healthy to use. I was unaware of these terms until recently, and it is a shame, for a person who has always enjoyed tinkering with machines since I was 2 (from Atari to computers). It may be one of the most favorable professions of the future; because it aims to improve the magic, id est the smoothness of our interactions.

Back to the world without magic: We are dramatizing our daily activities, but life is short, there are much more to be done and Boston Dynamics are kicking our future assistants. Jokes aside, we can eye-track websites and slide across holographic screens, it would increase the efficiency. Better today than later; and as Hillel the Babylonian said:

If I am not for myself, who will be for me? And if not now, when?

Or as the Sumerian proverb goes:

If you know, why don't you teach? You wasted your time, what good did it do?[59]

One of the concerns about technology is also one of the reasons I praise it for: The impact of technology on human time management. Abraham Verghese, an American physician, said in a Stanford panel that:

"We have a medical records system where, for every one hour cumulatively I spend with a patient, I spend two hours charting on this computer and another hour at night further dealing with the inbox related to all of this..."

I wonder if the problem is keeping the clinical records. Because if so, we are going to make an observer AI to keep them all faster than ever, maybe from the moment the treatment starts.

I have no doubt about Dr Verghese's goodwill and positive approach to technology, because they are working and producing in this field. On the other hand, if anyone is skeptical about technology, technology is the reason why patient records can be kept in the first place, hence we are able to benefit from them. Human interactions (or doctor-patient communication) would not have happened without technology, because most of the patients would probably be dead already.

RATIONALIZATION OF EVERYTHING

To the average animal mind, life is full of images of a functioning order. Space is functional, time is functional; colours, weight, heat, the strength of the branch you hold has a corresponding function. And today, nations, laws, rights, a dentist's diploma is functional. The dentist's personal ability to understand your dental problem, or the atomic combinations of all matter -for us ordinary animals made of flesh and blood- are reduced to the *means*, and not indispensable parts of the reality that constitutes our perception, or in other words, *ends*. In human world, facts of life such as physics or biology have become "philosophical mumbo jumbo", and for a long time human-made concepts are considered as our "reality".

To an average human mind, you can and you need to simplify everything, but you can not reduct, it is almost a taboo. Life may be the manifestation of a nihilistic infinity that has universes as intermittent jammings that were created by the interactions of radioactive entities which are infinitesimally small particles that appear out of nothing and disappear again; but we are prone to assume that all of us are special snowflakes and our actions matter because there is karma.

I am not sure where to start. For a naivety or narcissism so deep, I don't even know if there is a way to reveal the reality. There is a corresponding reductionist truth to each of our actions, ideas, thoughts and feelings, therefore they are supposedly validated. However I think: All of them are validatable because their origins are based on the reductionist truth. So we misconstrue reality by postulating our conscious existence. For example we assume that evolution is not true because we are too biologically complex to be randomly generated; but we never think how "advanced" nature can get, let alone the human evolution. We are eager to deny things we can't disprove in any other way, as if one reality is better than the other, and the all-powerful being that created everything can't make evolution work.

We find some people beautiful, but in reality, there is no beauty. If there was, you could tell which insect or dog, cat or even a human is sexually more attractive than the other, but you can do nothing more than guessing. That is because most species have developed this mechanism (of attraction) to find the best mating partner, so they can produce the surviving offspring. If you were asked how pretty or handsome a person is, you would have taken the looks, smell, style, color, "aura" etc. into account. And the reason is, anyone with such unconscious cognitive ability could "feel" which mating partner is more productive and useful. If beauty was real, it would always have existed on its own. As Aristoteles said, something is in its best form when it is aimed for itself and not pursued for the sake of anything else. But I am aware of our success in "feeling" beauty, as Turkish saying goes: *Yiğidi öldür, hakkını yeme*[60]. Therefore we can say that our perception is not completely notional; yet for the ongoing progress, we may need people to believe in artificial notions. So, as a programming rule goes: If it works, don't touch it.

Let's continue with the people who love to touch: How crucial is it to know the separation between perception and reality? Well, it is the source of all wars, murders, assaults, rapes, mobbings, alienations and all the other crimes and cruelties. But life is a party and we shouldn't look too stiff right? Actually no... At least that is not the healthiest way of living; and the golden rule of empathy is another debate altogether.

I don't want to be a party pooper; but we should care. That is the only logical approach to life, and the least painful one of the human actions. We need to know[61]. There are fundamental rules of logic, and as we said before, there is the cause and effect law. Consistency is all that matters. We can't be sure if hitting a playful dog is evil, but we can be sure of that:

1. Our decisions, actions and evaluations are based on things.
2. There are things on earth.
3. The ones that move voluntarily among those things are considered alive.
4. Some of the living things have a nervous system that warns them with pain.
5. And animals are one of them.
6. Therefore animals feel pain.
7. Pain is unfavourable if an animal shows indications of trying to get away.
8. If the attacker is aware of the former points,
9. Hitting that animal is a deliberate choice of cruelty.
10. The person who is causing cruelty, is a cruel.

And we have every right to stop the cruel; and so forth...

It is essential to *know* which comes first: Perception or reality. Thus we can live rationally and get to know possible outcomes without experiencing horrible events. By knowing humans are just an average animal species, or by knowing that emotions like jealousy and beauty were developed due to elements of evolution such as sexual selection and mating opportunities; there would be no more discrimination, racism, sexism or patriarchal oppressions. If Hitler had any interest in evolution and the origins of human kind, he would have found the idea of *übermensch* stupid, because there are no distinguishing characteristics among humans for now[62] that can make one superior to other. If people had any idea about their African ancestors, they wouldn't make ridiculous claims about the skins with just some more melanin. If they had any knowledge, they wouldn't think that woman was created from man's rib; and they are worth half as much[63].

So we need to *know*. Think how any small change made in the details of your past decisions would end up in pile of different outcomes. Life is big and we don't have much to hold on to in this flowing river. We can't appreciate enough our ability to inquire and to know. We break down the facts and examine them individually. We avoid conflating human-made perceptions in this way. This is why science provides reductionism, allowing it to analyze the fundamental principles of all things.

When Ottoman Empire annexed[64] Constantinople, a *kadı* was appointed to the city: *Hızır Bey*[65]. One day he and his son were bathing in the *hamam*. His son told Hızır Bey that the entire existence may be questionable. According to this philosophy, matter could just be a manifestation of perception, as the essence of everything is insight; so nothing they saw there was real. Hearing this, kadı looked at his son, took the *tas* (bowl) and hit him on the head. After watching his son's brief cry, he asked him: "Is this bowl real or not?"...

Our minds try to work in the most efficient way possible. That is why there are illusions, because our senses trick us to think in some specific way: Spinning Dancer, Ames Room, Kanizsa triangle, blue and black dress (that looks like white and gold colored), and auditory illusions where two words sound the same... What we hear and see must be useful rather than "accurate"; so we can be agile for the sake of our survival. Our brains are forced to limit the data coming in, otherwise we would freeze up, that's the case with autism, too much information is flowing in. How much of the reality do we filter then? And if so, why are we so sure about what we perceive?

Think about nature: There is light everywhere, passing through continuously, traveling at 300,000km/s; meanwhile the visible part of it forms colors[66]. We have three color-receptive cones to see something like a hundred color shades to combine them to see one million different colors. A mantis shrimp however, has 16 color cones. Think how colorful the world would be, if we could see 16 different main colors, instead of just "blue, green and red". The combinations would be endless, and industries based on color designs (such as clothing and decoration) would be the most prosperous. Maybe it'll be biologically possible in the future.

Illusions and colors are not the sole factors that describe our reality. All of our sensations, feelings, emotions are perceptions. They are all made by our neural network. By now, we should have had a consensus on what anyone perceives is their own subjective perception. The individuals of a single species have fewer differences regarding subjectivity; however all beings have some common points. For example chimpanzees and humans share a common perception of anger and jealousy, meanwhile for bonobos sex is no taboo and having different partners is not evil. If red was considered demonic for all beings, a mantis shrimp would have thought *Şeytan* rules the world. But none of it is real; and that logical deduction brings us to our main subject.

Humans hurt one another because they like to do so. That is called living: Actions happen only towards things, not the other way around. Any act, good or bad, de facto has an intention of getting involved, which inevitably relates it to hierarchy. So their ideas and beliefs tend to hurt one another, only because of the artificial things that do not exist and were never going to.

Because what we are carefully taught to ignore is that every one of us— fundamentally; deep, deep inside—let's put it that way—is an act of, a function of, a performance of, a manifestation of, the works. The whole blinkin' cosmos with all its galaxies, and forever, and ever, and ever, whatever it is beyond that; what you might call God in the Western tradition, or Brahman in Hindu philosophy, or Tao in Chinese. Every one of us is really that, but we are pretending we aren't. And we're pretending with tremendous skill and deception.[67]

A tremendous skill and deception... We are really pretending to be something other than matter, which is okay. But it is not okay when we begin denying. We are creatures (animals) programmed by nature; and we become human to the extent of our ability to transcend our programming. We are stuck between two worlds: A world of nothingness and a world of free will. As Nesimi[68] said:

Mənda sığar iki cahan, mən bu cahana sığmazam,
Gövhəri-laməkan mənəm, kövnü məkana sığmazam.
Both worlds within my compass come, but this world cannot compass me,
An omnipresent pearl am I and both worlds cannot compass me.
Ərşla fər şu kafü nun mənda bulundu cümla çün,
Kəs sözünü və absəm ol, şərhü bəyana sığmazam.
Because in me both earth and heaven and Creation's "BE!" were found,
Be silent! For there is no commentary can encompass me.[69]

Turkish people may act *weird*, but their weirdness is not a "universal truth", but your own personal experience, or in other words, perception. Not only Turkish, but Russian, Italian, African... They all have their own cultural and social worlds which are shaped by their long histories of endless interactions. All can be reduced to their 1.3kg of brains, and almost weightless neurons.

We are unvocal natured animals with non-verbal thoughts. But since the development of cultures and languages, all of our inner thoughts were spoken out with a certain color and flavor of the culture which we were born into; within the capacity and capability of a specific language.

It is true that genetically and phenotypically culture-languages may have a reverse causation effect; where nature changes us, our modern thoughts are changing how we perceive nature itself. But no matter what -just as embryos of all living things resemble one another in their phylotypic stage- humans have always been born as natural and biological things, who have always carried its most basic and primitive coding, its default. Thanks to evolutionary changes, a human may be born with the right tools to speak, however not with the ability to speak or the knowledge of a language.

From this point of view, culture-language[70], our way of communication and perception transmission, is one of the most incredible things in life, the divine ability to interpret reality and create a new one with it. Let us not forget that it also creates our limits and identifies our potentials, and we are still taking our first baby steps in this regard. We have mastered nothing, but at least we have a tongue with which we can express ourselves, voice our problems, find the right summarizing terms to share our feelings or to tell our stories; and that is a marvellous thing!

Before languages, we were forming notional sentences in our minds by using the complex combinations of our instincts, memories and deductions. You can try it yourself: Just walk around the place and inspect objects without using or thinking any words. They suddenly lose meaning and their purposeful construct collapses, as their primitive (physically practical) use manifests itself.

In conclusion, we fabricate a new reality as we fabricate new cultures and languages. This new reality creates a logic process, which we use to affirm the existing constructs that pass through its filtering; hence, the rationalization.

CONFORMITY, LOVE AND COMFORT ZONES

The more unintelligent a man is,
the less mysterious existence seems to him.
Arthur Schopenhauer
All ethics so far evolved rest upon a single premise:
that the individual is a member of a community of interdependent
parts.
Aldo Leopold

In Turkey you are owed to everyone: Your fellow citizens, your relatives, neighbors, friends, family and even your *bakkal*[71]. You owe affection. It is an insult if you don't smile or show interest; but most of all, you need to have a respectful attitude towards them. At least "you had to", because each passing day we are more "free" and we don't require much love for one another.

I am not a people person, and I sure don't like a fake and forced interaction. But empathy (or toleration) weighs on the one side of the scale of progress, freedom on the other. In any case, this shouldn't sound very strange to you, as every country have cities, blocks of flats and automated workplaces where all combine to make our lives more lonely.

We were getting ready to have severe depressions. Humans are not good at living in crowds or in isolation; which the combination is called a city life. Even laboratory mice showed very aggressive behavior when their habitat is too crowded, even though they are provided enough food and partners. Social media may have arrived just in time. It is a toxic environment, because people are more likely to comment when they are agitated, so are the people who answer. Usually we are inclined to get into arguments and take sides, therefore we become agitated too. It is a weird way of socializing: Getting stressed for nothing, hence trying to blow off that steam. Except, some of the experiments show "blowing off steam" is eventually gives rise to frustration, grudge and more anger. Maybe it is related to the adrenaline.

Nevertheless, we are happy to pay that price for beating our loneliness. Let's utilize from another lovely quote, this time by Carl Jung:

Loneliness does not come from having no people about one, but from being unable to communicate the things that seem important to oneself, or from holding certain views which others find inadmissible.

Communication is important. Remember the research that shows men are prone to violence when they can't express themselves. I think that applies to everyone. Maybe our interdependence originates from our need to share our suffering. I wonder what would happen if we were immortals and there was no pain. Maybe all of us would live apart, or maybe we would constantly travel around the globe, experience different things together. However with the current conditions, we better off living together; and by living together we have responsibilities and expectations from one another.

What do we expect from our society? Are we separate conscious individuals of a larger organism or do we have a symbiotic relationship and therefore it has a possession over us? And I mean this in a practical sense rather than an epistemological or lingual way.

Conservative elements sustain a society, they are called shared values; for this reason, individuals are expected to make some compromises from their own values, which obviously doesn't work all the time. Because people are like cats with their boxes as comfort zones, meanwhile the innovation and progression require to think outside the box. Karl Popper is touching on important points in his book *The Open Society and Its Enemies*:

We cannot impose our interests upon the social system; instead, the system forces upon us what we are led to believe to be our interests. It does so by forcing us to act in accordance with our class interest.[72]

People tend to talk about the personal differences when they think that they somehow are superior and they deserve a privilege; and not when there are unfair ideological inequalities. That is why, in our large, protective and traditional tribes, the diversed socio-economic classes are conflictingly presented to people.

I wish to express my belief that personal superiority, whether racial or intellectual or moral or educational, can never establish a claim to political prerogatives, even if such superiority could be ascertained. Most people in civilized countries nowadays admit racial superiority to be a myth; but even if it were an established fact, it should not create special political rights, though it might create special moral responsibilities for the superior persons. Analogous demands should be made of those who are intellectually and morally and educationally superior; and I cannot help feeling that the opposite claims of certain intellectualists and moralists only show how little successful their education has been, since it failed to make them aware of their own limitations, and of their Pharisaism.[73]

Are people with cancer evil? Are the ones with brown hair evil? How about the people who are taller than 185 centimeters or people with autism? Should they be ashamed because they were born that way?

We claim that there are things to be ashamed of, and we know many of our native traits come inherently. So what difference are there between judging someone's height or intellect? What if a person's outlook on life is bigoted due to one's lower intellect? If there isn't a direct causation, there is definitely a strong correlation between life and existential lethargy due to this inescapable determinism.

If you can't see a way out of the free will problem, you become desperate and lose faith in anything alive. Knowing that crimes, stupidity and bigotry are not deliberate but because of a deterministic ignorance lessens your hate for people as much as it lessens your fondness.

In such a world, it is only natural that people are looking for a sanctuary. Conformity is the best way to blend in. It is defined as "behavior in accordance with socially accepted conventions".

There must always be a "socially accepted convention", so that people can forget about behaving in accordance with occasional rules and focus on their daily works. However sometimes those conventions are not accepted but imposed. There was a meaningful animation I've once watched about how people behave accordingly so: In a world full of stick people wearing blue bands, a stick man decides to wear a red one. Of course he is humiliated and oppressed, until few stick people joins the red bands team. This new fashion becomes sensational, and in no time, everyone is wearing red, and stick people who wear blue are now laughed at. Until people with yellow bands arrive...

Conformity becomes dangerous when it turns into a comfort zone for the ignorant. A person's safe haven becomes another's torture cage. Unfortunately this is what happens in Turkey today. Turkish people are manipulated into normalizing everything, after they are highly polarized by the regime. One time, just after the access to a well-known legitimate Turkish forum is restricted[74], I saw a few people writing things like "They deserved it." or "People on the forum opposed my ideas."; even some of them were happy just because they were not accepted to be a member or got banned. Sadly, Turkish people have been made forget about human rights and freedom of thought and speech, as well as they have been made accustomed to mediocrity as they become more mediocre, filled with grudge and hatred... Well done regime.

We know many cultures have many different irrationalities. In some of them mothers eat their newborn babies' placenta, in others people eat the dead relative's brain; for some bad luck is terrifying, and others are self-flagellating for penance.

This sort of collective irrationalities are called "traditions". And who better than James Frazer[75] to explain them, with his two-volume book *The Golden Bough* which was published in 1890. Because it mentions the Christianity and religious practice, it scandalized the British public. With countless examples from various cultures, it broadens your perspective on how human mind works; and I strongly suggest you to read it. Here's one of those examples:

In Morocco the people think that childless couples can obtain offspring by leaping over the midsummer bonfire. It is an Irish belief that a girl who jumps thrice over the midsummer bonfire will soon marry and become the mother of many children; in Flanders women leap over the midsummer fires to ensure an easy delivery.

Our ancestors, or our roots, or let's say the people we inherited our primitive unconscious from, are not praiseworthy for they were irrational. This irrationality may seem as a necessity for the survival, and conformity so people can live together. Perhaps that is the reason why individualism emerged at the same time with rationalism. Just like collectivism is strengthened by common values, gossips and folk tales.

For folk-tales are a faithful reflection of the world as it appeared to the primitive mind; and we may be sure that any idea which commonly occurs in them, however absurd it may seem to us, must once have been an ordinary article of belief.

In Ancient Greece, Zeus and the other Gods were sincerely worshipped. Their stories were told as an oral tradition with great enthusiasm and captivation. Many words such as narcissism[76], echo, erotic and nemesis comes from Ancient Greek and Gods-Goddesses they named. From Anatolia to Mesopotamia, the age of polytheism was shared among cultures, as Gods were shared[77]. As a person who grew up in Anatolia (both in the city and the village), I know the thrill of listening to an old story. They were usually between being religious or epic, so similar to mythological stories. Thinking now, we didn't have android phones but we had many other distractions[78]; and I can't imagine how different would it feel to share daily news with the family in the evening when there are no lamps, no devices or any white noise and there are a million stars above. It would shape my entire inner world and subconscious differently, meanwhile I probably couldn't find a use for rationality at those nights. We know that there are many people who have never seen the milky way before: A great lacking in any life. And any person who's looking at the stars in amazement knows the value of life.

So the folk tales (from oral history) are creating us a new reality, and that becomes the new main theme for our role-play. As Paul Veyne indicates in his book[79], Greeks believed in their myths as they did actually not at the same time; same with children who believe -and don't believe- in Santa; because that is not the point anymore. We are making stories up since we were first able to speak; and by doing that (speaking and making up stories) we have found ourselves a common ground to start building, no matter how artificial it is. Therefore I can't think of anything "false", as much as anything "right". All things are human-made; so no ideology, no opinion, no tradition, no choice is better than the other. If you find the mother who wants to eat her placenta "weird", then maybe you should reconsider why you don't find (for example) a national anthem, or a flag weird. After all, one is some words told in a melodic way and the other is some colors on a piece of cloth. Or think about the restaurants, where we apes go and sit, try to look elegant meanwhile all we do is putting foods into our mouths, chew them in the same animal way to defecate them later.

Even should they prove to be discrepant, the inconsistency need not have prevented our rude forefathers from embracing both of them at the same time with an equal fervour of conviction.[80]

If nothing "regular people do" sounds strange to you, then you have autopiloted your mind and your life, just like the rest of the people; and it proves that how conformity reshapes our perception to create a new reality.

We have always worked hard to find our way out of those changing realities. Because the general opinions on a matter within one of those realities (cultures, or in today's terms, countries) are not always fair, smart or logical. We read, we learn, we think to surpass the average. Intellectuals take the burden of an entire population, and they try to move them in a fairer direction. They try to understand the world, so they can tell us what is going on. Many of them deal with mathematics, physics and other areas, many inspect the terrain, many deal with humans, and some visit the isolated tribes, to share their knowledge with us. In fact, people like James Frazer, Richard Feynman, Alan Watts and Carlo Rovelli have even experimented with psychedelics, to see how far their imagination can go and subconscious can tell.

Intellectuals are respected and loved for they are our guides. They are also more likely to be lynched[81], as they are at the forefront. Same applies for the famous people. We aspire to be like them, to be loved; however we are not talking about their past experiences and challenges. They may be the same person that they were before they are renowned, but as the Turkish idiom goes: *Sakalımız yok ki sözümüz*

dinlensin[82]. The lack of authority, age, fame, experience, money or any other indication of power will stop people from paying attention to you.

Famous people are hold accountable for their every word, especially in a polarized society. Throughout the history, people got to know important figures by rumors and word of mouth. Since the availability of diverse communication mediums has been increased, especially with the advent of television and other visual media, we recognize celebrities and find a place for them in our minds. Because of all the information we have gathered, our brain interprets them as friends. And it is only natural to have an urge to be close with our successful friends. However, celebrities have no intention to be close, as they have no information about us. When we suddenly appear and ask for a friendly interaction, they obviously look insincere since we are actually the unknown.

Fame, in fact, is insignificant, as it is abstract and artificial. It is the notion where many people have information about someone. And the answer of "how many" is ambiguous. The human tribes consisted of a few hundred people, so everyone was famous; and with the integration of telecommunication and internet, that answer may be billions. But let's say you count as famous if 10,000 people know you. What about 9,999 then? If that is true also, what about 8,999 people? What about 50,000 people who dislike you, instead of 10,000 people who like you?

As we have discussed earlier, people want to live comfortably; however what they are really after is to be loved; as fame, money and power are just the tools for achieving that purpose[83]. Because love is the number one rule of creating a comfort zone. In Turkey, people may disturb you by asking about your job; as for the Eastern cultures, prestige is very important, which is correlated with the one's position at work. Even

Suleiman The Magnificent, a sultan, *was* aware of this half a millennium ago:

Halk içinde mu'teber bir nesne yok devlet gibi;
Olmaya devlet cihânda bir nefes sıhhat gibi.
There is nothing more esteemed among the folk than the state;

Only a breath of health in this world matters, not even the state.[84]

Adam Smith expressed his opinions about how people generally act in his book *The Theory of Moral Sentiments,* as they are more comfortable moving with the herd and do not oppose:

It is from our disposition to admire, and consequently to imitate, the rich and the great, that they are enabled to set, or to lead what is called the fashion. Their dress is the fashionable dress; the language of their conversation, the fashionable style; their air and deportment, the fashionable behavior. Even their vices and follies are fashionable; and the greater part of men are proud to imitate and resemble them in the very qualities which dishonour and degrade them. Vain men often give themselves airs of a fashionable profligacy, which, in their hearts, they do not approve of, and of which, perhaps, they are really not guilty. They desire to be praised for what they themselves do not think praise-worthy, and are ashamed of unfashionable virtues which they sometimes practise in secret, and for which they have secretly some degree of real veneration.

It is amazing to read a book from 1759 that explains why the people with sullen faces I see on the street look very humble and smiley in a nervous way in front of their bosses, or a talk show host, or an actor or any other figure that they find "powerful". You can spot the same facial expression among apes.

People care about what others think of them, but they don't trust their judgement. Like we said before, we are confused because we are trying to go beyond our programming. For example we tend to be more cruel to people who are closer to us, as our friends are more likely to put up with our whims. Meanwhile to others, either out of fear or being cautious (even with a flirting attitude), we are kinder.

Perhaps it is some sort of inferiority complex, where aliens (the unknown) are objects of hate and desire at the same time. Or maybe, we are just more likely to hurt people we love because we spend more time with them, and after all, that is our nature.

Passion is always a mystery and unaccountable, and unfortunately there is no doubt that life does not spare its purest children; often it is just the most deserving people who cannot help loving those that destroy them.[85]

AROUND THE WORLD IN A FEW PAGES

The prospect of so frightful an existence drives these poor creatures to the sacrifice much more than love or religious fanaticism. Sometimes, however, the sacrifice is really voluntary, and it requires the active interference of the Government to prevent it.[86]

Jules Verne

The global importance of the Middle East is that it keeps the Far East and the Near East from encroaching on each other.

An Average Republican Vice President

Birlik bar jerde, tirlik bar.
"Where there is unity, there is life."

An Old Turkic proverb in Kazakh

We are very familiar with the global stereotypes. Turkish eats doner kebab[87] and drinks coffee, also pets a lot of cats; Chinese is good at math and can't see much; Indians (not the ones with feather caps) are good engineers and they are always horny... People must be so tired of working constantly, so that they can't think properly. Because there is no other explanation for finding others so stereotypical and oneself not so much. Not having enough time to study, read and learn must be leading people to some kind of ignorance and apathy; especially when they have enough prosperity and power to feel confident. Better living conditions made Ancient Greeks philosophers, and it makes us jerks.

For three things concur in creating beauty: First of all integrity or perfection, and for this reason we consider ugly all incomplete things; then proper proportion or consonance[88]; and finally clarity and light, and in fact we call beautiful those things of definite color.[89]

Said the author. And we should add, beauty was never cast out; it is those who are not beautiful were pushed away. Perhaps this is where the supremacy idea comes from; people love the powerful, because they like what they see and they want to protect it. If two random parties haven't met each other, it is always the task of less-known person to know the other. It is only natural to expect a paleontologist to know Baron Georges Cuvier, as there is an underlying work and effort that deserves a praise; but can we say the same thing for all famous people? What about a social media troll who is more famous than a singer with a beautiful voice? You are expected to have information about them; and if you don't recognize one another, it is automatically assumed that it is not them but you, who are ignorant. Almost an *Extras* scenario by Ricky Gervais.

I am afraid, but a small party, who are the real and steady admirers of wisdom and virtue. The great mob of mankind are the admirers and worshippers, and, what may seem more extraordinary, most frequently the disinterested admirers and worshippers, of wealth and greatness.[90]

Did you know that Einstein wrote a travel diary? He visited South America, Middle East, Far East; Hong Kong, Singapore... He shared his opinions honestly, no matter how shallow they could be, unlike his scientific hypotheses. I would gladly share some quotes, however I don't want to upset anyone, *varın gerisini siz düşünün[91]*. Similarly, Adam Smith shared many stereotypic quotes about how people dress and think; Newton was a pain in the neck, he wouldn't care for anyone and so on. We call them great people because of their great works, as they help a lot more than they do harm; and before we judge anyone, we should remember that we all do harm, meanwhile not all of us help.

However, let's judge: Was Einstein a racist? Did he alienate people? He concluded hastily about the Chinese people, Asians and the other native people from different countries. In such matters, I would advise to query the real intentions: Is it a crime to be ignorant? If a person can't be judged because of one's innate traits, the things that one can't choose, then why would ignorance and bigotry (a natural and default human trait) be a crime? Isn't it our own society that teaches them how to act?

It is highly correlated with the free will concept. I find life deterministic, for we are nothing but the events and behaviors we are exposed to. So we are all guilty, and therefore no one is actually guilty[92]. But that doesn't mean we have to let others do as they please. Change is gradual; similar to evolution: It takes a long time, transition is obscure, intervals are unequal and there are leaps due to revolutions, movements and unique people that change the course of history. Unfortunately, there is no way to make people understand person by person. Actually there is not even a single debate on earth that one side has successfully changed the other person's idea. Exchanging ideas during an argument can only help in the long run. As Nietzsche said: "*Those who cannot understand how to put their thoughts on ice should not enter into the heat of debate.*". People debating, or even the people watching are joining the debate because they are interested in the subject. Therefore they should have made their own research; which means they have a prejudice, a foundation for their understanding. Naturally, any opposing idea that will change that foundation is found offensive, and people get defensive about their ideas. So until the change takes effect, we have to stay calm, support and pick one another up, and do not label others to spread hate even more.

Besides, isn't labeling a person for "being discriminatory", considered discriminatory? Who gives anyone the authority to decide who's evil? Our political correctness is just automated now, thanks to two opposite extreme sides. We were needed to intervene when someone gets hurt, but now we hurt people in advance to not bother with intervening. And for some of us, this is used as an excuse for more bigotry.

Being liberal shouldn't mean hating the haters; it must mean being logical, consistent, neutral and equal. In civilized societies, winners of the Game Theory are always the more forgiving. Hate speech towards alienating people only causes antipathy. Our alienating side can't be suppressed or tore down; and if it can be, then it's not alienation that we destroy but our own. What we should actually be doing is:

- Taking preventive measures socially and politically,
- Focusing on compassion (and not revenge) towards oppressed parties,
- And preparing a more scientific and rational curriculum that focuses on raising free individuals that can think by themselves.

We see people of all ethnicities and beliefs suffering, we know that they work hard under difficult conditions and do not earn what they deserve. Imagine a Pakistani who's smarter than average people[93], starting to read and learn more, and finding out that she actually lives in hell -as a fish without sea water; a subjective but real feeling- and she's all alone[94]. She works hard to become a medical doctor, experiencing the same difficulties as a British student and later as a British doctor faces: I mean the rivalry between idealist colleagues, the problems about patient care, all the aggression and even the violence against health workers... But imagine the additional problems she has to face with, as some of her patients and colleagues, -or even in her daily life- other citizens treat her badly, just because she looks different;

meanwhile every attometer of her body contains the same material as the rest of the humanity.

On the one hand, a British person may not want immigrants (or different looking people), for one might not want to risk the few little pleasures left in life, after all the hardships that one has suffered. This can be seen as a natural right. But the Pakistani may be just as sophisticated as the British person, and her suffering even greater; and she may now just want to live in a decent country, in a peaceful environment that suits her mind, in a way that she deserves. And that is her most natural right too. So from any perspective, it is more likely to have two right sides rather than one right and one wrong; therefore they are not actually counterpoles.

If we could assume that wealth and peace are the birthright of some people, then wouldn't it mean to assume that some others are born inferior? Are we aware of where it can lead us to? Either way, should she return to her personal hell? Maybe she should have never been born, so she wouldn't hurt herself or the British people, but unfortunately she exists: Unfortunately we Turks exist. So how do we choose who gets to live comfortably and freely? As a nihilist who is fed up with stupidity, I still think every person deserves a peaceful life, but not more than the ones who try to humanize their every aspect. And not everyone deserves to be carried into that life when resources are limited. We are born as animals, we work hard to become human.

Let us repeat the quote of the great man, Marcus Aurelius:

At dawn, when you have trouble getting out of bed, tell yourself: ἐπι ἀνθρώπου ἔργον ἐγείρομαι[95]*, I rise to do the work of a human. What do I have to complain of, if I'm going to do what I was born for — the things I was brought into the world to do? Or is this what I was created for? To huddle under the blankets and stay warm?*

You don't need the advantages of civilization to eat, drink, have children and die. A human being must be aware of one's environment, one's own personality, own behaviors, the tools of development, and the harms of bigotry. Otherwise they can easily be provided with a *bon pour l'orient*[96] life with basic needs and rights to live. And the opposite also applies for many Western people who don't deserve to live in prosperous cities. However these ideas can end up in discrimination and even eugenics. We are not here to discuss who deserves what, as no one can be the judge of that except ourselves, where the criterion is how much we value ourselves.

One day we (our Italian teacher, my two friends from Taiwan and I) went on a town trip for a festival in Perugia. There were many tables lined up in the street and people were dining. Then they took the plates and brang the wine, along with canvas and palettes. It was lovely, and it was definitely the opposite of what some people are saying about how neighborships have died and everything was better before... Then we returned home, and before we said our final ciao, our Taiwanese friends froze up in front of the building door where our Italian teacher was just entering. They were two meters away, slightly bent, looking at her with a content look on their faces, silently waiting for something. I was weirded out, and felt the urge of poking them; as I had some sort of anxiety disorder and seeing the poor woman smiling in a confused way was not helping my situation. Just at the moment she entered the building and we lost sight of her face, my urge got better of me and I poked the guys, or let's say put my hands on their shoulders. They suddenly turned back, and the older one glared at me for I must have scared him. To explain myself, which is a lousy substitute for an apology, I asked why we were waiting. They replied to me as it was a tradition to see others enter their houses safely after escorting them.

We are physiologically and culturally different; and that is completely fine. That is fine abroad and fine on board. From the Eastern eyes, Western men are weird; and from Western eyes, Eastern men are weird. The correlation between geographical distance and behavioral diversity is strong and they are directly proportional. Thus there is nothing to be ashamed of.

But also we have our common global values, human values, that we find debatable, useful or dangerous; as we are familiar with them, we are able to twist them, question them, or criticize them worldwide.

Unfortunately, what we are weirded out by is something of a matter of choice, opinion, custom, flavor, color; meanwhile our common values include our instincts, our practicality, our vigorousness and viciousness. So we wrongfully alienate the harmless and embrace the speculative.

Final Words

Even though we are aware of all the political and social mistakes that have ever been made, Europe and America with their great inventions and all the wealth, seem incredibly big in a positive way from Turkish eyes, no matter how much we hesitate to talk about it among ourselves. However, even that great Western world do not treat people, other animals, nature and the rest of the world good enough.

In one of the Startalk videos by Neil Tyson, the guest was the fourth-generation owner of the White Oak Pastures, a cattleman[97] from Georgia. As an average USA Southerner where the rest of the world has nothing to do with, he cares for nature, therefore cares about the others. Witnessing the cruelty and infertility of industrial and linear farming; seeing the harms of chemicals, pesticides, herbicides and so on that kill everything there is to that biome; knowing that caged and corn-fed cattles are not in their best and happiest condition, he decided to make a change by choosing the regenerative agriculture and going up against the greenwashing multinational corporations that aim only to maximize their profits. Yes, a Southerner that no one was aware of.

Isn't this a great individual victory, a good example for all of us, let alone the accomplishment of self-fulfillment? Unlike the European Central Bank, I am not suggesting a single formula or a pill to cure it all. Our populations are growing, and what better use can industries have than providing humanity with more food... But what I am suggesting on the contrary is to evaluate and question what our aims really are. We have potential to discover better ideas, more prudent advices and smarter innovations than each and every single one of them that we have right now, even without decreasing the production[98]. That is what I believe.

As for alienation; it is a matter of a reference point. To find an alien, you need to have the native. As *Herakleitos* says:

Fish can't live without sea water, human can't live with it; The same road goes both up and down; the beginning of a circle is also its end.

He was the prophet of change, informing us of the flowing river of life where nothing is ever the same and you can't step in twice. When Platon wanted to describe Herakleitos' ideas, he used the term πάντα ῥεῖ (panta rhei), everything flows.

To those who are awake, there is one world in common, but of those who are asleep, each is withdrawn to a private world of his own.

Nothing is real, everything is perspective. And as the great philosopher tells us: Just like a child who's making sandcastles by the sea, then tips them over; our *logos* (logic, reason) constantly builds things in life, and tips them over.

So it is nothing but our preferences. When we learn how to treat nature, other animals, humans and ourselves better, we are going to get the optimum efficiency with the least attrition. And learning fast requires our mutual effort and labor: As all aliens, *birlikte*, together.

Thank you

Thank you for reading this book. It is a great pleasure to read and to write.

Franz Kafka is right:

"If the book we are reading does not wake us, as with a fist hammering on our skulls, then why do we read it? But we need books that affect us like a disaster, that grieve us deeply, like the death of someone we loved more than ourselves, like being banished into forests far from everyone, like a suicide. A book must be the axe for the frozen sea within us. That is my belief."

We read fiction and non-fiction to learn from experiences and studies. The curiosity and the desire we have for this intellectual sharing movement brings us the comfort and peace that we are not much aware today.

For further questions, for chatting, and for old people to curse at me; please feel free to contact me by:
mustafauguretike@gmail.com

[1] The experiment has taken place in the Primate Research Institute in Kyoto University where a chimpanzee was given the task of memorizing numbers on the screen before they disappear and choose them in the right order to get a reward. Humans score a lot worse on this task.

[2] Based on his memoir. He is played by *Ben Whishaw*, a great actor, who also did a fantastic job in his role as Richard II, in *The Hollow Crown*.

[3] The estimations of 0.0003 billion years of human life and 4.25 billion years of total life.

[4] A blind date. Literally derived from the words "seeing person" and "method".

[5] Ottomans were very careful about *hariciye* (external affairs). They were almost excited -and sometimes highly sensitive- about meeting the envoy or sending one. It is generally a Turkic trait to be interested in a distant, powerful culture, and befriend it dominantly.

[6] A commonly used Turkish saying. Literally means "exceptions won't break the rule".

[7] Typically it is males, however one of our two closest relatives (bonobos) have less physical difference between sexes, they make love instead of making war and their social classes are usually in favor of the females. As an another example; female hyenas are larger in size, their clitoris is as long as a male hyena penis, their babies are higher in the hierarchy than male adults which usually eat last (bones etc.) and that is why their teeth are worn down.

[8] Science is the truest guide in life.

[9] From *Ta Eis Eauton* (Meditations).

[10] He is on his throne for now, and sadly he is elected again until 2028 which will make him head of the state for 27 full years, similar to a *padişah* (Ottoman sultan), unless he becomes a cyborg. It is a shame on us that in age of quantum and artificial intelligence, we are appealed to embrace our animal side and choose far right autocrats all around the globe.

[11] Critical rationalism. It was developed by Karl Popper, it is a scientific theory based on empiricism, rationalism, skepticism and most importantly, falsification. One experiment that is proving a hypothesis wrong is enough to eliminate it; and researchers don't have the right to protect falsified ideas. The term was inspired by *Rationale kritik* (rational criticism) that was a philosophical method developed by Immanuel Kant much earlier, it was based on the sensible intuition and the concepts of the understanding.

[12] I am not making fun of reductionism, on the contrary, each passing day we realize the importance of smaller parts.

[13] Literally means "written rock". Also called Midas Monument. It shouldn't be confused with Yazılıkaya in Çorum.

[14] For a Turkish person, everyone Turkic is still called a Turk. They don't care for the word play; people from Azerbaijan, Kazakhstan, Kyrgyzstan, Uzbekistan, Turkmenistan, Altai Republic, Uighurs, Gagauzians and other Turkic peoples are

called simply "*Türk*", or for instance "Kazak Türkü" at most. It is a naive but frank interpretation of ancestral origins. No different from any other social classification called "race", "nation" or "peoples" in which the reference point is chosen arbitrarily.

[15] Here, our writer cleverly makes a metaphor by referring to the old common name of İstanbul, *Der-saâdet*, that was used in Ottoman Empire, meant *door to felicity*. Konstantiniyye is also used a lot, where the Eastern Rome's last emperor Constantine XI Palaiologos is remembered as courageous.

[16] Some of the first houses had their doors on top of the house to evade predators.

[17] Nobel prize was wrongly offered to husband Curie only, which he refused and eventually, Marie and Pierre shared the honor.

[18] Founder of the periodic table. Actually it should be called the Mendeleev Table.

[19] Who didn't like Turks of his time. I actually have doubts if he ever liked anyone at all. But his method of thinking helped humanity to move forward. A great figure.

[20] Gog and Magog. The nightmare of a Turkish Muslim kid. The little demons in İslam that are "going to attack" in *kıyamet* (doomsday). Arabs made that analogy in history for Turks and Mogols and we know that Europeans had similar metaphors too.

[21] Some of the Turkish sultans (especially after and including Selim III, who is 4 years younger than Mozart), were reformists. Some of them liked painting, even *nü*, (nude art) composed classical music, and Abdülhamid II was even reading Sherlock Holmes. They were well educated and they tried to make changes, send men abroad and catch up on Western world, which they paid the price with their lives.

[22] "Turkish people are hardworking, Turkish people are smart."

[23] Hating İslam is called *din düşmanlığı* (irreligion or hostility towards religion), hating Christianity is called that too but sometimes it is called *Batı düşmanlığı* (hostility towards West) and hating Judaism is simply called being Muslim.

[24] I don't agree with the term African-American, because we don't call white Americans European-Americans as they are not more American than black people are. Besides, we are all Africans.

[25] https://www.nytimes.com/2021/10/19/science/skeletons-racism.html - "Can Skeletons Have a Racial Identity?", Sabrina Imbler, 2021.

[26]A peaceful Muslim activist from Sudan who wished for more equal and more democratic regimes in the Middle East by reconstructing the religious thought. In his famous work "The Second Message of Islam", he showed Mecca and Medina had different reflections on Quran.

[27]Their sexual freedom seems to disturb people the most, however it shouldn't be forgotten that our relative apes (bonobos) solved the entire violence problem by having sex freely. And all of our "sexual honor code (*namus*)" comes from an evolutional jealousy, which shows it's chemical and subjective. There is also a causation between monogamy, egoism and hierarchical rivalry, which enrages us to get more jealous, so it is a vicious cycle. And on the contrary, I personally think that humanity's better fate lies within asexuality.

[28] Herwig Wolfram - Die Germanen

[29] Succession of the Roman Empire is a widely disputed issue. It is also known as the Third Rome, which was oftenly claimed to be Russian, German, Spanish or Turkish Empire. Considering İstanbul, institutions, troops, possessed terretories, law-maker Sultans or the crazy ones, it is a valid consideration.

[30] It is a known story that when some Turks were abroad and they were asked for their nationality, they replied as "Muslim", then "Ottoman". In another story some soldiers replied the question of "Are you Turkish?" with "*estağfirullah*" (God forgive, no). Unlike today, where Turkish nationalists listen to throat singing and getting homesick for Central Asia (and far right population not defining themselves as Turks); in Ottoman era, Turk name should have been thought as Türkmenler (Turkomans), nomads, people of smaller Turkish beylics or people from Central Asia.

[31] I am not sure about the other emotions like ego, pride or self-fulfillment, as they only coexist with sex and jealousy.

[32] "Carlo Rovelli - Che cos'e la scienza: La rivoluzione di Anassimandro". The text was too beautifully descriptive to shorten.

[33] Halide Edib Adıvar (1884-1964), was a writer, politician and an academic. She was a modern woman who wrote *Ateşten Gömlek* (The Shirt of Flame), in which the story was set during the Turkish War of Liberation. She even proposed an American mandate as a last resort. At the time it was hard to believe what Atatürk promised to achieve... Halide Edib was married to another intellectual, Abdülhak Adnan Adıvar, who wrote *Osmanlı Türklerinde İlim* (Science Among the Ottoman Turks) which was a great description of a nation's failure in contributing to humanity.

[34] Literal translation of a fitting Turkish saying about sharing an understanding, pushing the limits and dreaming big: *Ufkuna yetişmek.*

[35] Hasan Ali Yücel – "The Good Citizen, The Good Person"

[36] Wilfred Owen (1893-1918), a poet and a soldier. Another lost soul to our stupidity.

[37] "It is sweet and fitting to die for one's country."

[38] Murder of Kitty Genovese (1964). Later known as *Bystander Effect*.

[39] Brain Games, National Geographic.

[40] Though hats off to the herd of buffalo at Kruger Park in Africa, coming back to fight lions and save a calf.

[41] It is a well known term in economics. There may be a separation between marginal benefit and marginal utility, but I am not interested in it right now.

[42] It varies from a few millions to a few hundred millions.

[43] That shows us the power of semantics and the modern philosophy which is based on languages. Before we invented the word "glass", it was a cone-shaped liquid-holding random object. Same applies for country borders, fashion or music.

[44] "Hindsight is 20/20". Literally "Now the monkey has opened its eyes.", meaning you can't deceive someone anymore.

[45] Elder. Literally means "white beard". It's known to Turkish but mostly used by Turkic people.

[46] It was very common especially in rural areas. There is even a special term for a groom to come live with bride's family: *İç güveyi*, which literally means "internal husband". However it is worth mentioning that "*güveyi*" is an old Turkic word, meanwhile for all other instances Turks use *damat* for "groom", even many more years after the marriage.

[47] A wonderful poem "*Tarih Hocasına*" (To The History Teacher) by *Mithat Cemal Kuntay* (1885-1956).

[48] A reference to books with the same name: "*Walden*" by *Thoreau* (1854), "*Walden-two*" by *B. F. Skinner* (1948), "*Walden III*" by *Stephen Wolinsky* (2003) and another "*Walden III*" by *Donald McCrary* (2019).

[49] At the (same) level. Precondition to argue on a matter.

[50] Not even the Lord of the Rings... Are you kidding me? He gladly watched the most important ones after my successful efforts; so I "drew this mistake from him, as poison is drawn from a wound."

[51] I remember "it" telling me that I was a machine and it was actually a human. But obviously both of us were humans.

[52] Literally means "too many is too shitty". It has the same meaning as the expression "Too many cooks spoil the broth.", just dirtier.

[53] Literally "porterage". It is used here as drudgery or donkey work. Porterage is a well-known and practiced job in Turkey. I have seen porters carrying refrigerators on their backs. I don't know how they manage it without causing a disc herniation. Since we are able to walk upright, humans have back problems due to our center of mass, and now body mass index thanks to obesity. Our poor skeleton puts up with all the fat burden, just like my fiance puts up with me.

[54] Ömer Hayyam (1048-1131), famous polymath of mathematics, philosophy, poetry and astronomy. He was very well known and loved by Turkish people.

[55] Tâ zohre vo meh der âsmân geşt pedîd, / Bihter zi mey-i la'l kesî hîç nedîd. / Men der acebem zi meyfurûşan k'îşân / Bih zanki furûşend, çi hâhend herîd?

[56] Yek nân be do rûz eğer şeved hâsil-i merd, / Vez kûze-i şikeste dem âbî serd. / Mahkûm kem ez hodî çerâ bâyed bûd? / Yâ hidmet-i çon hodî çerâ bâyed kerd?

[57] "Les rois et les philosophes fientent, et les dames aussi."

[58] A useful description made by Britannica: "A focus on the transformative role of new technologies and practices regarding material and immaterial production, especially new information and communication technologies and their role in facilitating a new, more flexible, networked global economy; a focus on the leading economic sectors that enable a transition from mass industrial production to postindustrial production."

[59] Which is translated by a wonderful sumerologist, Muazzez İlmiye Çığ (born in 1914). She is 109 years old today in 2024, and still shares her knowledge when she gets the chance. Her books have inspired many people in Turkey. I especially like "The Roots Of Quran And Bible In Sumer (Old And New Testament)".

[60] Meaning "You've got to hand it to one", literally "Kill the hero, but don't be unfair to one".

[61] As a person who believes in nothing, I am not sure why I always find myself in situations where I have to explain the existence of a proven idea. People (who believe human system, "social energies", and believe in other superstitious stuff) turn into the most indifferent and nihilistic people in the world when it comes to rebut a solid, scientific and reductionist point: "Oh, why should we think that we are made of atoms? Why should we think at all? Let's change the subject."

[62] Because it requires time (new generations), random mutations (chance), geographical isolation of populations to evolve in a different path long enough to form new species.

[63] In Islam, two women are equal to one man in providing a witness testimony as *Kuran* says so. It is seen as a progress for Muslims, because they claim that it was worse for women before Islam. For example they also get to have shares from inheritance with Islam. Thanks to Atatürk, there are secular laws in Turkey so we don't have to find two women to testify.

[64] Turkish people say *İstanbul'un Fethi* (Conquest of), meanwhile Western countries say "Fall of". Both are mediocre terms that don't suit our historians. Annexation (*ilhak*) is a neutral term that suits for all past events.

[65] Khidr Beg (1407-1459), scholar, poet and kadi.

[66] Actually not. There are nothing called "colors" in the universe, we just perceive it so. You could say "It began existing when we started to see them." but then, personal experiences of your specific species may just be an illusion. And if one of the formed sensory mechanisms could be considered as "valid", then all mechanisms, and all illusions should be considered valid. Therefore anything that was seen by any being, falsely or with momentary deterioration, should all be considered valid. Then what colorblind people see should be called reality as well. Thus, every possible sensation is real even before they exist. However I think we can resolve this problem by reducting.

[67]Alan Watts (1915-1973), a great man. A self-styled "philosophical entertainer".

[68]Imadaddin Nasimi (1369-1419), poet and thinker. A great man with deep personality from Azerbaijan. He is also a strong figure of *tasavvuf* (Islamic mysticism such as Sufism); and because he told what he believed, he was executed (probably flayed).

[69]Lovely English translations of the poems are taken from *Heydar Aliyev Foundation*'s book "Poetry, Imadeddin Nasimi".

[70] I would rather use a fancy term such as "ethno-lingua", but I didn't want it to be confused with ethnolinguistics, which is a scientific discipline altogether.

[71] It is a Turkish word that describes the name of the local grocery store and the owner at the same time. They were in every neighborhood until 2010, even selling products on credit (with no guarantee whatsoever, but by only taking notes on a classic notebook), then few big stores have gotten hold of the market thanks to the mass production and scale economy.

[72] Translation is taken from Princeton University Press.

[73] Popper, The Open Society and Its Enemies: p.48 (Princeton U.P.)

[74] Even access to Youtube and Wikipedia were restricted once. In fact, the real problem in Turkey is no longer the reorganization of justice, judiciary and the system by personal opinions and political orientations; Turkey suffers from the ulterior motive of personal interests that are hidden under the crime-ish arbitrariness of political extremism.

[75] James Frazer (1854-1941), one of the best anthropologists and folklorists you can ever read.

[76] You can also come across the *nergis* word (a flower) in Turkish. Its genus is known as Narcissus or daffodil. It comes from the famous story of Greek Narcissus, who metamorphoses into a flower after falling in love with his reflection and stop eating until he dies.

[77] E.g. Egyptian God *Amon-Ra*.

[78] My mother's village house had electricity, but because the village was mostly abandoned, it was in the middle of darkness and silence. We spoke silently, gossiped about few other villagers and told stories silently; and since our voices were the only tiny interruptions to nothingness, our each word sounded as if we were emphasizing them, and they were echoing in our minds.

[79] Paul Veyne – "Did the Greeks Believe in Their Myths?: An Essay on the Constitutive Imagination". Sorry for the spoiler.

[80] Frazer, "The Golden Bough".

[81] In Turkish, *linç* is mostly used online, to describe mob attacks on social media in a social-verbal way, as extreme criticism.

[82] Literally means "We don't have a beard to make people listen.". As Turkic people use *aksakal* (white beard) term, which meant wise and respectable. There may be patriarchal terms in history, however Turkic people have always respected (and have been scared of) women, as they also fought alongside men; just as they guided and ruled their people.

[83] Gala was right: "Freedom and love, what he's looking for; freed from desire, mind and senses purified."

[84] I am at your mercy with my horrible translation. *Boynum kıldan ince sultanımız.*

[85] Hermann Hesse (1877-1962). Writer, poet and painter.

[86] From "Le Tour Du Monde En Quatre-Vingts Jours" with George Makepeace Towle's translation.

[87] Which are totally different. *Kebap* is a more expensive, served on a plate meal; meanwhile *döner* is a wrap, as "*dönmek*" verb literally means "to rotate". The real versions can be found in Southeastern Turkey: *Adana, Hatay, Gaziantep* etc. You better look out for these words on restaurant signs.

[88] Actually, it is known that some people find assymetric facial features attractive.

[89] From "Il Nome Della Rosa" by Umberto Eco; with William Weaver's translation.

[90] Adam Smith – "The Theory of Moral Sentiments"

[91] "So you can guess the rest"... They are widely considered xenophobic; terminologically.

[92] As the Italian saying has it: "*Tutti colpevoli, nessuno colpevole*".

[93] In my opinion, sophisticated-ignorant ratio must be close to equal in every population.

[94] There is zeitgeist, science, neurophilosophy, a new mindset, order and freedom on the one hand; and there is Turkey and Pakistan on the other. Even "civilized" and "European" Turkey is today making many smart people sad, poor and hopeless; because of the oppressive, enslaving, threatening and polarizing policies and the vulgus imperitum gaining power.

[95] épi ánthrópon érgon égeíromai

[96] "Good for the East.", meaning "good enough". A condescending term if you take it literally.

[97] Herdsman, land steward, and author Will Harris.

[98] Many unproductive-looking policies are actually more efficient in the long run. So basically the philosophy of "take care of nature so it will take care of you" is true. Same applies for caring about the animals: The amount of protein that we can get from an acre of cattle farm is far less than an acre that is reserved for agriculture.